REACHING the PEAK

How I Climbed to the Top in Network Marketing
(and How You Can, Too!)

JEFF ALTGILBERS

Published by

SHORT BOOKS. BIG IDEAS.

Success in 100 Pages

www.SuccessIn100Pages.com

ISBN 978-1-947814-89-9

Copyright © 2019

All rights reserved.

"Only those who will risk going too far can possibly find out how far they can go."

— *T.S. Eliot*

"A bad day on the top of the mountain is better than a good day in the valley."

— *Jeff Altgilbers*

FOREWORD BY
RAY HIGDON

P eople say it's impossible to "motivate" others—that all motivation comes from within.

They haven't met Jeff Altgilbers.

An eight-figure income earner with over 700,000 distributors in 57 countries in his downline, Jeff not only inspires others to be the best they can be through his words—he is the ultimate *"leader's leader"* who changes people through his actions.

What makes Jeff Altgilbers most interesting, however, is his story—a story you'll learn in the pages to follow.

Jeff's climb to peak success didn't come easy or fast. He endured years of struggle and poverty, but he didn't give up on his dream of being more and having more.

There is no *quit* in him.

Today, Jeff is one of the top income earners in the world of network marketing, having helped multiple people become millionaires in his downline. He has spoken all over the world, sharing his message and inspiring people to follow in his path.

A few years ago, Jeff joined our private training and mastermind group, *Top Earner Club*. And it became quickly obvious that Jeff was the real deal.

Most importantly, he was there to learn. He was like a sponge, soaking up knowledge with a deep desire to grow—which is exactly what it takes to be successful in this profession.

As a result of his involvement in TEC, I can honestly say that Jeff is one of the most impressive, authentic human beings I have ever met. But with all the success Jeff has achieved, he is most proud of his wife and kids.

In September 2017, my wife Jessica and I were building our dream house in Ft. Myers, Fla. Then we heard hurricane Irma was forming in the Gulf of Mexico and bearing down on us—and our dream.

And as much as we wanted to stay in Florida, it became clear the safest thing to do was to clear out. We decided to head up to Tennessee and wait out the storm. To our surprise and great gratitude, Jeff and his wife were nice enough to open up their home to all attendees and threw an epic party for a group of people who he mostly didn't even know.

During this time, my wife and I got to know not just Jeff but his entire family better, all within the context of his home, family and friends. We learned exactly why Jeff raved about his family so much—why they made him so proud. Ultimately, we built a stronger appreciation for Jeff, built a greater connection, and discovered that in terms of qualities, it was his genuine love for family and friends that we really admired, appreciated and valued. And that is the Jeff we know and love!

For my money, the best way to truly know someone is through their family. My family will long remember the time we got to spend with his.

—Ray Higdon

P.S. I'd long-encouraged Jeff to write a book, to share his unique story, and perspectives on what it takes to achieve success in network marketing. I'm glad he's finally done it. And you will be, too.

"It is not the mountain we conquer but ourselves."

– Sir Edmund Hillary

INTRODUCTION

A Quick Word Before We Start Climbing...

It was in 1978, I was a struggling 22-year-old young man. I was earning money washing windows and cleaning carpets in Jasper, Tenn. I was pretty disillusioned about the future. Jimmy Carter was president, and the country was in a recession. My future seemed hopeless until a man introduced me to something I had never heard of.

It was a business model called multilevel marketing.

He told me if I got good at selling, could sell a case of product each month, and get other people to do the same, I could be earning some very good money.

Looking back, I try to remember exactly what my thought process was at that moment, what drew me in. Was it the product? No. The company had a product called aloe-vera juice, which was something I had never heard of. Was it the subtle way in which I was approached? Perhaps. All I can tell you is I had the three main ingredients all successful people in this profession have.

- First, I was open to the opportunity—any opportunity—and willing to listen.
- Second, I was ready to make more of myself and to do more with my life.
- Third, I had nothing to lose.

So, I said yes and went for it—and thank God I did. Because that one decision launched me on a path that became more than a career—it became a life I once only dreamt of.

This is why, to this day, I believe anyone who's been throwing around the idea of getting involved in a home-based business should take the plunge, if for no other reason than the personal growth and development that comes from the experience.

Is Network Marketing Right for Everyone?

Without a doubt, the network marketing profession provides people with many benefits, chief among them:

- Escaping the rat race of working in a typical 9 to 5 job and being your own boss.
- The freedom and flexibility to live, work and travel wherever you want, whenever you want.
- More time to spend with the people who matter most to you.
- The ability to work with people you want to work with (and not have to work with people you *don't* want to work with).
- Low start-up costs, compared to virtually any other business, and numerous tax advantages.

- The pride of doing something new and building something from the ground up.

- Plus, a number of other benefits I won't take the time to list here.

So, taking all this into consideration, and having achieved a dream-level of financial freedom for myself and my family, there's a natural temptation to answer the above question with an immediate and enthusiastic, *"Yes."*

The truthful answer to this question is:

No.

Network marketing is *not* right for everyone. But, being a business owner provides an opportunity for growth that cannot be achieved in almost any other way. As the saying goes, "You are either building your future or helping someone else build theirs."

Jobs Are No Longer the "Safe Path"

There are many people who are reluctant to take the entrepreneurial route of building something on their own. I understand this. Finding a good job, being an employee, and working for someone else, seems like the "safe" path. It's not.

I see this as the biggest flaw in most people's thinking.

The truth is, being an employee is the riskiest thing any person can do—especially in the world today. There was a time years ago when people could dedicate themselves to a single company, when loyalty between an employer and an employee was a two-way street.

Those days are gone.

Having your own business puts you in control of your future, which is wildly important when you think about where technology and a number of uncontrollable factors are leading us.

Why I Wrote This Book

Many people assume authors write books for one of the following reasons:

- *To make money*
- *To achieve fame*
- *To get recognition*

In my case, I've written this book for none of the above.

I've earned enough money, thanks to this profession, to take care of myself and my family for the rest of our lives.

When it comes to fame, count me out. I like the quiet life I'm living just as it is.

And, while the recognition of becoming a "bestselling author" would be nice (assuming enough copies of the book end up being sold), that's not the reason I've put my knowledge on paper, either.

I wrote this book for one reason and one reason only:

I wrote it for you.

Jeff Altgilbers

Gatlinburg, Tenn., USA
June 2019

"*Everybody wants to reach the peak, but there is no growth on the top of a mountain. It is in the valley that we slog through the lush grass and rich soil, learning and becoming what enables us to summit life's next peak.*"

– Andy Andrews

PART ONE:

Once Upon a Time in the "Stone Age"

I launched my network marketing career in a time that probably sounds like the Stone Age for many people reading this book.

And in many ways, it was.

The average income for an American was $17,000 a year, and the typical house sold for $55,000. A first-class stamp cost 13 cents, and a pack of cigarettes would run you 20 cents. I started before computers were *personal* and there was one in every home, let alone small enough to sit in your lap.

We had this device called a VCR where you could load a VHS tape and watch a professional presentation done by someone in our upline. We just sat there and sipped coffee while the prospect watched it, then we asked if they had any questions.

For group presentations, we used a slide projector. Even the thought of using slide projectors to make presentations makes me giggle, it seems so archaic and ridiculous now.

Cell phones were the new thing, too. They were gigantic devices that looked like walkie-talkies with an antenna (google "Michael Douglas Wall Street beach scene and you'll see what I mean). So when I would go into a restaurant and set my phone on the table, everyone would look at me and ask, "What do you do?" It was always an object to open conversations with and it was great when traveling because I no longer had to use payphone booths to make calls to verify the prospect was going to be home.

Of course, the internet and social media didn't exist.

Did this put people who wanted to make a living in network marketing (which was still referred to a "multilevel marketing" back then) at a disadvantage compared to today? No. Not really.

It wasn't a worse time to be in the profession. It was simply a *different* time. And many of the lessons I learned during those early years—*the years before we were all "connected"*—were very valuable, and they have served me well to this day.

In the Early Days

One of the phrases we used to describe our first *rank* back when I started was *"garage qualified,"* meaning we had to stock inventory of products not just for ourselves but also for our distributors. Our downline distributors would pick them up from us, and then deliver them to their customers.

That was the way it was done years ago. Scheduling pickups and deliveries was a difficult and often time-consuming ordeal. Today, with orders delivered from the company warehouse directly to the customer, the business is a breeze.

Another thing that was a pain in the neck was that the company would pay upline distributors for product, and it was then that person's responsibility to cut checks for all the people they sponsored. There was no such thing as each distributor being paid directly via direct deposit. And there was no back-room "dashboard" reporting.

Also in those early days, there was a far greater focus on selling products than there is today. Sure, the big money is and will always be made by sponsoring others, but product sales are critical, too. After all, no product sales = no income for anyone. As such, my activity was very sales focused when I started, and everyone in the business was taught to get others selling products. The concept of *remote teambuilding* was not something anyone focused on because there was no technology to support it.

Yes, today many things are easier. The amount of support provided by organizations is night and day different than it was years ago, which is a huge benefit for distributors, especially when it comes to time savings. Because every minute saved on distribution and customer service is a minute that can be spent marketing. After all, time is money.

Perhaps the best thing about technology is that it's made it possible for anyone to build a team on a local, national or international basis. Or, if you want, you can do all three, as I have done (a large part of my still-growing team is spread across Asia, which I will talk more about later).

The Power of Personal Interaction

I'm not telling you all this simply to walk down memory lane and reminisce about the good old days. (As I mentioned, some of the "good old days" weren't all that good.) It's to make the point that, while things move faster and easier these days, I'm not sure everything is necessarily better.

Why?

Because doing the business back in the Stone Age required lots of person-to-person contact. There was more face-to-face dealings and more talking on the phone. Things were more personal. Today, much of the *personal interaction* that existed is gone—not entirely, but a lot of it has been lost—which is a shame.

I say this not because I long for the past but because I've come to believe these connections, or "touch-points." are critical to the long-term success of growing and maintaining a productive team.

Operating From "Lack" Mentality

I got married at the age of 22 and ran my multi-level marketing business on a part-time basis for 14 years. Eventually, we had two children, and my focus was on being a responsible father, building a house, and surviving in my business. And that's what I did. That's *all* I did.

I survived.

Looking back, I realize the primary reason I didn't reach my full potential in those early days was due to limited, disempowering beliefs. I never considered myself worthy of anything greater then what I had at the time.

My First Mentor

To improve both myself and my business, I purchased cassette tapes from Nightingale-Conant, listening to them hours each day. One of my favorites was called "The Strangest Secret," written and recorded by one of the greatest motivators of all time, Earl Nightingale. I listened to that program so many times that it's fair to say Earl Nightingale was my first mentor.

I continued to purchase cassette programs and listen to them as I drove my truck from my house to wherever I had cleaning jobs. My wife would ridicule me for spending money on these cassette programs and say, *"Why are you wasting money buying those cassettes? How is that going to help you clean floors better?"* My answer was, *"It won't help me clean a floor better, but when I listen to them it makes me feel better."*

What I didn't realize was that getting coached from a mentor like Earl Nightingale was preparing me for something much greater than the life I was living.

Just listening to Earl Nightingale opened my mind to "possibility thinking" that helped me grow my imagination and gave me confidence that I could be successful in business.

I learned how to think as a leader. And how to talk like a leader. Before, I was emotionally insecure, and it was hard for me to come out of that insecurity. Earl showed me the door, and on the other side was a different me.

Opportunity Knocks

One day, out of the blue, I got a call from a friend. This person was someone for whom I had a great deal of respect because he was very successful. He said, *"I have something I want to show you."*

I said, *"Is there money to be made?"*

He said, *"Yes, lots of money."*

I told him, *"Then you better get over here in a hurry."* Needless to say, I was open to hearing what he had to share.

The next day he pulled into my driveway, got out of his Mercedes, and went to his trunk. I can still remember standing there, watching as he pulled out a water filter. *"That's what you came here to show me? A water filter? There's big money to be made with that?"*

He laughed and said, *"I'm taking you to an event in Nashville, and then you'll understand."*

My Eyes Were Opened

When I went to that meeting in Nashville with my friend, I was shocked to see there were thousands of people there. This really blew my mind.

Over the next couple of hours, I watched different speakers take the stage and talk about how they were earning as much as $50,000 a month in the business. After the main speaker finished, I turned to my friend and said, *"Let me get this straight. That person up there sponsored some people, who sponsored other people, and all of the people in this room are on his team? And he gets paid on all these people, but he doesn't have to pay them to work for him?"*

He said, *"That's right."*

I said, *"Well, then count me in."*

I was tired of hiring and firing people in my cleaning business and having to roll out of bed late at night when they didn't show up for work. That event opened my eyes.

Until then, I had spent most of my energy on my cleaning business and selling product. And while selling product made me decent money, it became clear that the big money—*the life-changing kind of money I wanted to earn*—was in building a team of people who also sold product. I understood the opportunity I was being shown was a system... one that allowed people to become wealthy because it provided the ability to leverage the work and efforts of others.

My Shift to Team-Building

When I first started, one of my challenges was I didn't have much of a warm market. (Note: For those of you who are brand-new to the profession of network marketing, your "warm market" is defined as the people you already know—in other words, friends, family and co-workers.)

And I realized this business depends on people tapping into that warm market to sell products and sponsor people. So what was I going to do?

Well, as the saying goes, *"You don't know what you don't know, so go find someone who does."*

So, I decided I needed to go to someone who knew: *my upline.* I reached out to those above me for advice and learned from them how to reach a lot of people through advertising.

They taught a system of running generic attractive ads that would appeal to people who want to be *"job free"* and earn serious money. This was a huge shift for me, which required a very different approach from the one I had been using.

Talking to Strangers

It was 1988 when I started advertising. I met up with people I had never known in restaurants and coffee shops, then together we opened an office in downtown Huntsville, Ala., just over the Tennessee border.

Ironically, Rick Springfield had a hit song a few years earlier called, "Don't Talk to Strangers," which played on the radio all the time. It was not the message I needed ringing in my head because now, for the first time, I was *offering the franchise* (the business model) *to strangers* (as opposed to only my warm market).

And it changed everything.

If you want to achieve financial freedom and live the life of your dreams, you must become comfortable talking to strangers. This is not optional. *You must.*

Grant Cardone, author of the bestselling book, "The 10X Rule," puts it extremely well when he says, *"The truth is you need to talk to strangers because strangers have everything you want. Think about it. If you're not talking to strangers, you aren't going anyplace in your life."*

He's right. If you're not willing to talk to strangers, you can say goodbye to a wealthy future.

Getting the Phone to Ring

The goal of running ads was simply to get the phone to ring. (Remember, there was no social media or email in those days.) Fortunately, the advertising approach worked, and that's what happened. The task now was to get good at handing the calls.

One of the challenges I faced—something that *all* network marketers face to this day—was having people ask, *"What's this about?"* To which I learned to respond: *"It's going to be much better if I show you in person rather than trying to explain it over the phone."*

Next, without hesitation, I would then say, *"I have openings at 10 a.m., 1 p.m., or 7 p.m. Which of these would work best for you?"*

In the world of sales, they call the "alternative choice" a "close," a technique that's been around forever. And something that works like magic. Using this approach, I would line up my presentations for the week, which kept me and my other leaders quite busy.

(FYI: I use the term "leader/leaders" to describe anyone who has joined my team for the purposes of building a network

marketing business, not the number of people they've sponsored or their current ability to lead others.)

"Climb the mountain so you can see the world, not so the world can see you."

—McCullough

PART TWO:

Challenging Times Lay Ahead

As the 1980s were coming to an end, with a new decade in front of me, I faced some challenging times in my personal life.

As I mentioned earlier, I'd gotten married when I was in my early 20s. Truth be told, we were both young, but we weren't in love—not *true* love, anyway—and it showed up in many ways. Our needs were so different. We'd had kids together, and I loved my children very much. Being a part of my children's lives was very important to me. But divorce was inevitable.

At the same time, my cleaning business was dependent on two major accounts. Unfortunately, in 1991, I received some very bad news from both companies: They were terminating my services because they needed to save money.

I had built a very strong business for 10 years and suddenly was faced with no money coming in.

Living alone in Huntsville, Ala., I only had one account left—a large retail store. My total gross income, before expenses, was $500 a week, which I gave to my ex-wife to support my children.

At the same time, my multilevel marketing business had also experienced setbacks. The company I was with offered high-quality water filters, which was great for my customers, but created a problem for me. Why? This kind of product failed to provide for any sustainable or substantial residual income because there wasn't any consumption or replacement.

To make matters worse, many leaders in my upline had encouraged people to purchase large inventories of product. Today, we call this "front-loading." Which is a really bad business practice. Not only is it a bad practice, it got on the news. This gave the company I was with a bad name, and many people left the organization.

My income disappeared overnight, and I was forced to do something I never thought possible—I declared bankruptcy. What I didn't know at the time was that losing my businesses— both the cleaning business and my network marketing business—was the best thing that ever happened to me.

Embracing Adversity

Even the darkest cloud has a silver lining if you look hard enough for it. In my case, losing those businesses and the income from them created in me a sort of fire, helping make me unstoppable.

Until then, I had been playing small.

I discovered there was a much bigger person hiding inside me, just waiting to emerge. It took walking through the fire of adversity to bring it out.

So first, I started selling off the equipment left over from my bankrupt cleaning business and used that money to live on. I needed to buy enough time to figure out what I wanted to do next. After having had employees for the past 10 years, I knew I did not want to go down that road again. I also knew I would never be happy working in a job as an employee for someone else. I had dreams and knew I didn't want to work in a service business trading time for money.

Some might say I was lost. Did I feel sorry for myself? Was I down and out? Sure. But looking back, this was all part of finding my way.

After spending a full year feeling directionless, I decided to clear my mind by spending the few dollars I had left on a weekend trip to Gatlinburg, Tenn.

Gaining Clarity in Gatlinburg

In case you're unfamiliar with Gatlinburg, it's a popular tourist destination on the edge of the Smokey Mountains in Eastern Tennessee. In addition to the standard hotels and other attractions, it has a 407-foot Space Needle observation tower and a 2.1-mile aerial cable car that lets you ride from the town to the top of the mountain.

My reason for choosing Gatlinburg wasn't because of the touristy things—it was because I was going through a lot of emotional storms and was a place my father used to bring our family on vacations when I was a kid.

And it was there—sitting on a park bench in Gatlinburg, staring up at the tree-covered mountains—that I finally knew what I needed to do.

Sitting there, on that bench in Gatlinburg, I thought to myself, *"What is wrong with you? You have been teaching and telling people for years about the financial and time freedom that can be achieved through multi-level marketing. You've listened to Earl Nightingale for hundreds of hours and know you can have any life you want. What's wrong with you?"*

Making the Decision to Succeed

I realized that, during my first 14 years in the profession, I'd treated my multi-level marketing business as a hobby. It was just something I did for extra money. I liked being in front of groups doing trainings. And I loved playing the "role" as a leader. But had I ever really *become* a leader, a true leader who got the most from myself and others?

No.

There were people in my upline who'd made fortunes, but I hadn't applied myself and taken the business seriously like they had. I had only been playing with it. I'd flirted with it. But I'd never committed myself to it. I'd never made the decision to succeed. The big question was, *why?*

Why hadn't I committed?

As I look back on it now, I see that because of the income from my cleaning business, my ability to support myself had never depended on the money I made from my network marketing business. Now, with my back against the wall, I had only two choices:

- A life of struggle, embarrassment and lack, or...
- A life of wealth, personal pride and freedom.

Those were my choices. My only choices. Period. I'd experienced a life of struggle, and that was no longer acceptable. It was time to decide. Do it or don't do it.

I decided to commit to a new start.

Digging Out From Under

At this point, the money I'd lived on from selling off the cleaning business equipment was gone. And, in terms of recruiting a team of leaders, I was starting over there, too. The team I'd built in my previous opportunity had scattered, quit or we're not interested in beginning again. But at least I knew the direction I wanted to go.

Network marketing was the best path for achieving the time and financial freedoms I wanted for myself. However, I needed to find the right company for me. This, in and of itself, was an interesting change from the last time I'd gotten involved in the profession. The previous time, I'd been approached by someone with an opportunity.

All I had to do was say, *yes*.

This go-round, I found myself in the driver's seat, proactively searching for a company to join.

On a quest of sorts, I decided on the following "must have" criteria:

- The company needed to have been in business for a while (ideally five years or longer) and have a reputation for high integrity.

- The company needed to have great sales and recruiting materials. (I wasn't expecting the company to provide free materials because this was *my* business, but I wanted to know they *had* great materials to use.)

- The company's compensation plan needed to be attractive and simple (as opposed to pay plans that require people to have a PhD to understand).

(Note: Today, were I starting over, I would have added the importance of having a great marketing *system* that took full advantage of current technology.)

The other thing I knew for sure was that the products needed to be highly consumable, goods or services people would re-order month after month (which was not the case with the water purifiers). And the products had to be something I could get excited about and have fun with.

My Search for the Right Company

I got a copy of USA Today, where many networkers placed ads, and answered over 100 of them. To my great surprise, only 10 of them sent me information! I was shocked by this. Why would anyone spend money advertising, then not respond to the leads?

In any case, of the 10 companies that *had* responded, one sent me a VHS tape (for those who don't know what a VHS tape is, Google it). It was a weight loss product, a cleansing tea, and—though the tape itself was pretty goofy—I felt the product could be a good fit. It really fascinated me.

The package included an application signed by the woman who had sent it. It had her signature and ID number on it, so assumedly she would be my sponsor.

I waited for her to call me. She didn't.

I decided I'd give her one more week to call me—one week, no more.

She never called.

It was important to me that whoever's team I joined, the person had to be a responsive leader. In the past, I had been in companies where they just signed you and left you, and there was no training, and they were never there when you needed them. I was not going to make that mistake again.

It was clear that if this woman couldn't follow up with a lead—someone who had responded to an ad and shown interest in the product—she would not be there to support me when I needed her. I liked the company, but there was no way I would allow her to be my sponsor.

I called that company and asked them for the name and phone number of the number-one income earner of that company. The man's name was Ken Pontius, and he already was earning hundreds of thousands of dollars a month.

I called Ken and when I told him I wanted to join direct to him, he told me he was not taking any more frontline leaders. I told him, *"Well it looks like you're going to miss out on a lot of money, aren't you?"*

And that's all it took. He quickly changed his mind and became my sponsor.

The Biggest Mistake People Make

There's a lesson to be learned from my search for a company all those years ago, one I hope is not lost on you. And the lesson is this:

> *Had the woman I initially contacted followed up with me, she would've made a fortune. But because she was either lazy or not committed or not interested, she gave that fortune to someone else.*

Looking back now, years later, I've calculated that the woman's lack of responsiveness and follow-up cost her several million dollars.

And this, I believe, is the top reason people fail in network marketing. They get a lead but never follow up.

"I'm Broke, I'm Broke, I'm Broke"

In March 1993, after discovering the company I was looking for (as well as the right sponsor), I still had a problem. I had no money to get started. I barely had enough to live on. And to make matters worse, I'd just written a check for the distributor kit, but there was no money in my bank account! Miraculously,

I managed to get the $35 I needed into the account in the nick of time, and the check cleared. However, now I found myself with no money to buy products.

Needless to say, I experienced a lot of anxiety and a lot of fear about my future, wondering how I was going to get the money to get started.

One day I went outside and sat on my porch, lowered my head, and I prayed. I sat there thinking, *"I'm broke, I'm broke, I'm broke,"* over and over again.

Then suddenly, I heard a voice.

And no, it wasn't God (at least I don't think it was) because the voice was my own. And the voice said: *"Will you just shut up! We know you're broke! Let's go do something about it!"*

Doing What You Can, With What You've Got

When I lifted my head, sitting there on the porch, I looked out and saw the only thing that was left from my bankrupt cleaning company, sitting there on the driveway.

A truck.

Not a nice new truck, either, but an old *junker*. The engine didn't start, and one of the tires was flat. The only thing the truck had been useful for had been the fact that I'd kept one of the windows rolled down for a neighborhood cat, so he could sleep in it.

"This is my answer!" I thought. *"This junk truck is my ticket out of here!"*

I grabbed my phone book (yes, we still used phone books in those days), found the number for the local junkyard, and dialed the number. Explaining the situation, I asked the man if he'd come out and tell me what the truck was worth.

The man from the junkyard arrived, looked the truck over, and in an apologetic tone said, *"All I can offer you is $400, but that's it."*

I can't begin to tell you how overjoyed I was at that moment. He may have thought $400 wasn't a lot, but to me it was a Godsend. After he paid me and towed away the truck, I took $200 and bought groceries for the house. Then I used the other $200 to buy products, so I could get started building my business.

I was not going to sell my life out for an excuse. I could feel I had much more potential that I hadn't yet tapped and I was going to find out who that man (me!) was. And I have never looked back.

Since that day in March 1993, I have earned $26 million in my network marketing business. You might say I literally turned a piece of unwanted *"junk"* into a life worth living.

Problems Versus Circumstances

It amazes me that people will throw away their future and settle for nothing. They remain in a state of want, a state of scarcity, because they just accept their circumstances.

When someone's reason (translation: *excuse*) to not join my opportunity is to tell me they're broke, I always say: *"I understand you're broke, but what's the problem?"*

Without exception, the person will respond by saying, *"I just told you I'm broke."* In doing so, they've set themselves up for a thought redirect. I will say, *"No, that's not your problem—that's your circumstance. What I'm asking is, what's holding you back from getting started?"*

Being broke is never a reason for not moving forward in life—if anything, it should be the reason *to* move forward and *fix* the circumstances.

Sell some junk. Have a yard sale. List that precious flat-screen TV on Craigslist. Do whatever you have to so you can get started on building the life you've imagined.

The thing I wonder is, if we sell our future out for some B.S. excuse, how can we ever look our children in the eyes again?

Pain Is a Great Motivator

I remember one such painful experience with my son, Micah, when he was two years old. After picking him up from my ex-wife for the weekend, I wanted to make sure we'd have a great weekend. So I stopped at the grocery store on the way back to buy his favorite food. Unfortunately, the store was a place where (though I'd always made good on my debts) I had bounced checks.

After getting the groceries, as I was exiting the store, the manager came up and grabbed my shopping cart. He got in my face and said, *"No, you're not getting these groceries!"* Then he handed me back my check. I was so humiliated. It was bad enough that such a thing was happening period, even worse it was playing out in front of my son. I felt worthless.

That said, the pain created from this experience became an additional driving force. I vowed I would never let my son experience anything like that ever again. I would pay the price and do whatever it took to become successful.

Building a Prospect List

My focus sharpened on prospecting. I knew a lot of people who I could approach with my new opportunity, but I hadn't taken the time to make a list. I needed to get their names on paper because until something is on paper (or in a document in a computer), it isn't real. And until it's real, nothing is going to happen.

So, I made my list, then got immediately to the task of contacting the people on it. Procrastination was out of the question since I had no money and there was no time to lose. I didn't wait, I got right to it.

Where Are You Calling From?

Because I was still broke, I could not afford a cell phone, so my sponsor graciously lent me one. When I discovered I could not get reception where I lived, I drove up in the hills of Tennessee where I could get reception and made phone calls from there.

One day, as I drove in the hills, high into farm country, I opened a cattle gate and pulled my truck over to where the cows were grazing. I closed the gate behind me so the cattle couldn't get out. Then I put my prospecting list on the hood of the truck and started calling the prospects on my list.

During my prospecting calls, people could hear the cows mooing in the background and would ask, *"Where are you calling from?"* I would reply, *"Oh I'm out for a drive in the country, just enjoying nature."* They had no idea that my office was a cattle ranch, my desk was the hood of my car, and that I was surrounded by cows and piles of manure.

When I'd get someone to agree to meet with me, I would drive and meet them in restaurants or their homes—wherever I could find a free place for us to chat. Paying rent to have a "hotel meeting" was out of the question. Heck, I barely had enough money for gas and two cups of coffee. Sometimes I would have to borrow money to get the gas to drive back home!

None of it was perfect, but it was good enough.

It was good enough.

I was not going let a few small *inconveniences* get in my way, no matter how embarrassing the situation appeared. My desire to escape my circumstances—and to achieve success—had made me unstoppable.

*"Life is like a mountain—hard to climb, but the view
is worth the effort."*

— Anonymous

PART THREE:

Not Out of the Woods
Quite Yet

Though I'd gotten off to a good start and had a group of people to work with, I was still broke. So I took jobs cleaning carpets during the day for a company, and some nights I was cleaning grocery store floors.

I was three months behind on my truck payments, and on my utility bills, too. Then, one day, there was a knock on my door. It was a man from the utility company coming to collect. He told me that if I didn't pay the past due utilities, they would have to cut them off.

I told him, *"Sure, I can write you a check for the utilities. My checkbook is in my truck in the driveway. Let's go out to my truck, and I'll write you a check."*

When I walked outside, I saw that the driveway was empty. My truck was gone! The bank had come and taken it away in the middle of the night—with my checkbook in it.

Now, with no utilities and my truck repossessed, I found myself once again asking, *"What am I going to do now?"* As painful as it was, I knew I was going to once again borrow money.

I had an old friend, an 80-year-old man who had joined me in the business. He was a retired engineer and graciously gave me the money to get my utilities back on and loaned me a car that looked like it had been in his family four generations. It had almost no paint left on it. The car was so embarrassingly ugly that when I went to meet with prospects at coffee shops, I would park several blocks away, far from their view. Still, I persevered. Once again, quitting simply wasn't an option.

The Road to Success Is Bumpy

One day, I had to do a meeting in Cincinnati, which meant I'd have to drive this old, borrowed car 300 miles there and another

300 miles back. To be honest, I wasn't sure the car had 600 miles left in it.

To play things safe, I went to a mechanic to look it over and had the oil changed. What I didn't know was the mechanic had failed to tighten down the oil filter lid, so oil was spewing out the entire way up the interstate.

As I was driving, I was thinking that things were finally coming together. I had a growing downline and felt everything I'd dreamed of was going to come true.

Then I heard a noise coming from under my hood. The oil gauge had dropped to zero. Moments later, there was a loud bang, and suddenly I found myself on the side of the interstate standing next to a borrowed, broken-down car. I had a major problem on my hands.

But I also had a thumb.

The Hardest Call to Make

Since my only asset was my thumb, I used it to *thumb a ride* with a trucker who took me to the next exit where I found a payphone to do something extremely difficult.

I called my father.

This was a hard thing to do because my family—my mother, father, two brothers and my sister, had all been talking about how my life had gone down the toilet. I had been doing great for over 10 years with my cleaning business, but now I'd gone bankrupt and had sunken to the lowest place possible—I'd gotten involved in one of those *pyramid schemes*.

But it wasn't a pyramid scheme. My father, in particular, simply did not understand network marketing. It wasn't something his generation had grown up with.

My father served in the Navy, then went to a university and got a degree in business. My two brothers and sister also went to universities and got formal educations. So that was the way my family believed it was done, and to do it differently was only frowned upon.

When I called my father and told him my car had broken down on the freeway, his only reply was, *"Son, I think it's about time you got a real job."*

I love my family very much. But they simply didn't understand.

Getting Back to Zero

When I got back home, my answering machine had 100 messages on it. *"Wow!"* I thought. *"The meeting has worked!"* Actually, they were all calls from creditors wanting their money.

A friend, who was with me at the house, asked, *"Jeff, what are you going to do?"* What could I do? I walked up, unplugged the answering machine, then plugged it back in. The message light went back to zero.

"Look," I said, *"Problem solved."*

The problem wasn't solved, of course—but there was nothing I could do about it in that moment. Calling bill collectors back to tell them I *still* didn't have their money would prove nothing. Even worse, it would be a waste of time.

In that moment, I realized that time was my greatest, and perhaps only, resource. Which wasn't true.

I did have other resources, including drive, desire, creativity—and, as I had just demonstrated by unplugging the phone to make the light go back to zero—I still had a sense of humor. In those days, I had to have a sense of humor, or I would have probably found a bridge and jumped.

The Past Does Not Determine the Future

Those days were not easy. I learned you have to build yourself first. I was still working on me.

I remember finding a way to scrape up enough to money to purchase the "Unlimited Power" cassette program by Tony Robbins, listening to it day and night, taking notes and studying what he was sharing.

Because I had so much past failure replaying in my mind, it was challenging for me to think I could be worthy of the great future Tony was saying was possible. Was I simply setting myself up for more pain and disappointment? I wasn't sure.

Here's what I *did* know. The things I'd done in the past had not gotten me where I wanted to be. So I could listen to the negative inner voice of doubt in my head, or I could listen to the positive, reassuring voice on the tape.

I chose the latter.

Though I was still forced to go out every morning cleaning carpets and taking additional jobs on the nights when I didn't have meetings to do, I kept a positive attitude. If Tony Robbins could go from being broke in a 400-square-foot apartment, doing his dishes in the bathtub, I decided it was possible for me, too.

Taking the Final "Leap"

By listening to positive motivational messages, combined with massive action, I grew my network marketing income to almost $5,000 per month. The life I dreamed of was finally starting to take shape—*it was becoming real.* (It was also due in large part to my 90-Day Plan, which I will give detail on later in this book.)

But I knew that if I was going to become *great* in the profession of network marketing, I'd have to let go of my cleaning jobs and take a leap of faith.

I wanted to go on a road trip for an entire month personally visiting people in my downline—people who, in many cases, I had never met, in towns and cities to which I'd never traveled. But doing so meant I'd have to quit my cleaning jobs.

Did I have what it took to commit? To really commit to my network marketing business full time and go after success with everything I had? I needed to find out. So I did it.

I quit my cleaning jobs and hit the road.

Hitting the Road

I traveled to Nashville first, then on to Ohio to do more meetings. Next, I headed further north.

My car at the time was a small Chrysler Omni with very little space in it, so I had to put my large charts with the company compensation plan in the back window. It was the only place they would fit.

The good news was everyone on the highway could read it. The bad news was it impossible for me to see out the rear window. But that didn't matter—I wasn't going backward, I was going forward. Everything I wanted was in front of me now.

When I got to the Canadian border on my way to do a meeting in Montreal, the immigration man looked at the compensation chart through the back window and told me to pull over. I was detained for several hours until he understood what I was doing, then he finally let me go.

When I'd finished my meetings in Montreal, I continued on to do more meetings in other parts of Quebec, then on to Nova Scotia and finally to Maine, where a large team had been growing.

In Maine, there was an amazing woman named Priscilla Smith, who I had called from a list of names I was given. Priscilla became my greatest leader, and she kept me there for weeks, doing meetings in homes, churches, schools, hotels and public buildings all throughout Maine.

My leap of faith had become an adventure.

Doing Versus Hoping

Leaving Maine, I headed south to New Hampshire, where I did a meeting for another leader, then finally down to Virginia to finish the last leg of my journey before going home.

I had been on the road for an entire month, and when I got home, the check from my network marketing business was in my mailbox. I was shocked to see my income had almost doubled.

It was funny, thinking about all the time I'd spent waiting for things to change. Hoping things would get better. Wanting success without necessarily doing the work. Now I was doing the work, and things were starting to happen.

Starting to happen.

I was earning money now, and I didn't have to split my time between building my team and cleaning floors to pay the bills. But I wasn't financially free.

The Fear of Losing What I'd Gained

As things began to finally start working for me, I found myself experiencing something for the first time, which was the fear it wouldn't last. Of losing what I'd gained, what I'd finally achieved.

I found myself replaying the negative experiences of my life in my mind and was terrified to go back to those dark days. To deal with it, I turned to my mentors on cassette again: Earl, Tony, and others whose ideas, clarity and wisdom kept me focused on where I was going, not where I'd been.

Another thing I did to stay focused on the direction I was heading was to go to a place I called Dream Street, which was a neighborhood where all the rich people lived in Huntsville.

On Sundays, I would drive to Huntsville, park my car, and go for long walks past the large pre-Civil War mansions. As I would stroll the streets, gazing at the homes with their big white pillars and sprawling manicured lawns and rose gardens, I would tell myself:

> *"Yes, this is the way it's going to be. This is how my life is going to turn out. The house with the pillars out front—yeah, I'm going to have a house like that, with rose gardens, yes—I'm going to have that and a gardener, too! And that Mercedes in the driveway, I'm going to have that and a BMW!"*

It's important to mention here that I did this long before I had money. I did this when I had no money, when I was totally broke, because even when you have nothing you can still dream.

But now, even as things were starting to work out for me, I realized how important it was to keep visualizing the life that was possible for me.

Did all this visualization work?

Yes.

In 18 months, I went from being penniless, walking among other people's dream homes and moving into the house of *my* dreams.

My Dream Becomes a Reality

My dream house (or should I say, my *first* dream house) was a Greek revival built in 1860 located in Camden, S.C. It had the pillars out front, just as I'd seen on Dream Street, and after I moved in, one of the first things I did was to have a gardener put in a garden with perennials and roses.

The reason I'd chosen Camden was because so much of America's history had started there. The town had a Revolutionary War park where two major battles had been fought, and eight confederate generals came from that town during the Civil War.

It wasn't long before I found myself not only being immersed in learning about Camden's history but also being a part of a unique community of people. I went to plays, attended performances of string ensembles and Broadway musicals, and was finally, really enjoying life.

I spent years restoring that neglected historic house back to its grander. A man by the name of Bob Allen, who'd worked on other historic houses in the area helped me. He even published a book of historic houses in the community and included mine.

For the first time, living in my dream home in Camden, I felt like I was somebody—and that I could contribute something and be a central part of a community. And get this: During the holidays, the Camden Junior League asked if I would allow *my* house to be part of a candlelight tour of historic houses. It seemed impossible, but I was a respected homeowner in a town that valued American culture and history—*my* house was now a home on *someone else's* mental street of dreams.

Visualization works.

(Side Note: Today, people call all the visualization I was doing the *Law of Attraction*, based on the premise that what you think about, comes about—*visualization* leads to *manifestation*. Looking back now, I can tell you that all the visualization I'd done at that time had only gotten me half the way there. It wasn't until I got into *action* that the Law of Attraction began to work for me. *Visualization* without *action* is worthless. Sorry, it's just a fact.)

Success Is Not Final

After five years of living in my dream home and enjoying the fruits of my labors, I received word that the network marketing company I was involved in was being sold. Worse still, the new owners didn't have any experience in network marketing.

What kind of changes would they make? I wondered. *Would the changes be good for the company, or would they be bad?*

At that time in 1997, network marketing was going through a compensation-plan revolution of sorts, largely due to advancements in technology. Technology also created radical changes in the way products were inventoried and shipped to distributors.

To make a long story short, the new owners of our company did not keep pace with the way other network marketing companies were doing business—in particular with the requirements within the compensation plan. In fact, they went the other way and made things worse. As a result, they made it virtually impossible to compete. This was devastating to me.

It felt like déjà vu, being overwhelmed by the same feelings I had when I lost my cleaning business years earlier and had no money coming in. Was I going to lose my dream house? Go back to the job market? Give up on my financial independence in network marketing goals?

The Decision to Change Companies

I knew I had a narrow window of time in which to take action. Sadly, that action was to join a different company. And that's exactly what I did.

The last time I'd joined a network marketing company, I'd taken my time, doing lots of research in the process. This time around, I didn't have that luxury and was forced to make a quick decision—which turned out to be a mistake.

The company I joined was involved in telecommunications but after a short period of time, I could see it was not a good fit, so I made the decision to find another company, where—within a relatively short period of time—I became the top income earner.

More Challenges Ahead

Though I'd hit the number-one spot in my new company, it didn't mean things were smooth sailing. There were still challenges to tackle, one of which was the new owners' failure to utilize the latest software to track sales volume for people's commission checks. People weren't getting paid on time. Some weren't getting paid at all.

I traveled to the home office to confront the owner. While I was there, I discovered a large room stacked to the ceiling with storage boxes. *"What are these?"* I asked.

The owner said, *"They're applications that haven't been entered into the computer yet."* I almost died! I had become the top leader in a company that had some serious problems.

The owner reassured me that he was working on fixing the problem, saying there was another software company he was going to use. I warned him he had one chance to get it fixed—there could be no more delays in paying our leaders. He gave me his word the problem would be fixed.

Sadly, the problem wasn't fixed. And as much as I wanted things to work out with that company, it was clear that was impossible.

On a nationwide conference call, I announced to my team that it was over—that they should not send in any more applications to the company and should cancel any checks for applications that had recently been mailed. It was a very difficult thing to do, but it had to be done.

Integrity Is Everything

To me, leaving the company was not about money, it was an integrity issue. I was still getting paid—but many others were not. To continue leading people into believing they would be paid for their efforts when I knew they wouldn't, was morally wrong. To me, *integrity is everything.* If you don't have integrity, what's the point?

The following night, the owner held a nationwide conference call of his own and told everyone *I* was a liar, that everything would be fixed, and everyone would get paid.

My integrity was being put on trial in the most public of ways.

While the leaders on that second call were very happy to hear everything was okay, I held my ground. I warned people not to trust the owner, but they refused to listen.

Two months later, everyone learned the truth. I had been right.

The company closed.

"He who climbs upon the highest mountains laughs at all tragedies, real or imaginary."

— *Friedrich Nietzsche*

PART FOUR:

My Lowest Point Had Arrived

I didn't have time to get emotional and feel sorry for myself. If I wanted to keep the lifestyle I had come to enjoy, I had to find a new company. I had to keep searching.

While I hate to admit it (especially in print, here in this book), I'd reached the point where I'd begun to question network marketing as a viable path to financial freedom. I began to lose faith in people, in particular people who ran these large network marketing companies. I'd built several great teams, only to have them destroyed.

Mentally, I was burned out.

My disillusionment grew so much that one day, I got a phone call from a man I'd worked with years earlier, telling me about a new company with a unique, consumable health and nutrition product. The product was exactly what I'd been seeking. And the man was even someone I felt I could trust.

I didn't even bother to call him back!

"I Hate Network Marketing!"

To work through my frustration over my situation, I threw myself into manual labor and went to work re-painting the historic 1860 house I owned. I can remember being up on a ladder thinking, *"I hate network marketing. All these owners are dogs!"*

It was during this period that another friend, a young hippie-kind-of-guy, called me. He told me he'd just joined a company and wanted to tell me about it. He gave me an 800-hotline number to call.

I called the number, which had a doctor's message about the product. After I listened to that message, I had a gut feeling I'd struck gold. I also listened to several conference calls where people shared their story after using the product themselves, and I was totally convinced of its validity.

I called my friend back and told him, *"This is exactly what I've been looking for!"*

He said, *"Are you ready to get started?"*

I said no.

Even though the product was exactly what I'd been looking for, I still felt emotionally damaged from experiencing so many failed opportunities. While I knew I had what it took to be successful in network marketing, I simply didn't know if I could endure another failure. Would this company fail me, too? I didn't know if I could go through the possibility of more pain.

Yet I knew I had to do something.

Working Out My Anger

After passing on the opportunity my friend had called about, I just kept painting the house, thinking how hurt I was over all that had happened to me.

My friend called again. Again, I said, *"No"*—the anger of my disappointment still strong.

Then he called again. *"Are you ready to get started?"* I told him I'd think about it when I was done painting.

My friend called again and again. Every time my answer was the same: *"When I'm done painting!"*

"How long are you going to paint?" he asked me.

"It's a big house," I said.

Finally, on New Year's Eve, he called and asked me again. *"Jeff, are you ready to get started?"*

I told him, *"It's New Year's Eve. I'm going to go out tonight and drink, probably a lot. I'll start the business tomorrow."*

Working From "Eight to Faint"

The next morning, January 1, I put down my paintbrush and locked myself in my office. For the next 90 days, all I did was pound that phone. *I went from eight to faint.* Every day I would start at eight in the morning, and I wouldn't quit until late at night, until I collapsed, building a new team.

Now, you may be thinking, *"Well, it was easy for you, Jeff. You already had a team of people you could call to get started with."*

This is not the case.

I did not bring in *anyone* who was on my team in the past. Those people were all burned out and emotionally destroyed over the failures we'd experienced, just like I had been. I had to start all over again without a downline.

I advertised in newspapers and in network marketing magazines, and I purchased lists. I also called people whom I had talked to before but had *not* joined with me at the time. Some of them joined this time.

After 90 days, I sponsored a number of new leaders and grew my team to 800 members. My third check from the new opportunity was over $5,000, and I did it with a telephone and tenacity.

That was all I had, and it was enough.

There Are No Perfect Companies

After that 90-day run, I was very tired, but my non-stop pushing had set the speed for my team, and I had a new team to run with. And while I was able to create a new income for myself very quickly in the new company, I was still leery about things. I was still a bit shell-shocked from the companies that failed me in the past. A voice deep inside still kept asking: *Is this going to last?*

What finally got me out of this fear-filled state-of-mind? It was when I came to the inescapable conclusion that there are *no perfect companies* because all companies are created by, and made up of, *imperfect people.*

I realized I could feel sorry for myself, throw up my hands, and quit, using the excuse that network marketing doesn't work because there are some unscrupulous dishonest people in the marketplace. And while this is clearly true, the greater truth is that unscrupulous dishonest people exist in *all* industries. The only question I had to ask was:

> ***Which was better—working for myself,***
> ***even in a potentially-flawed network***
> ***marketing company, or working as an***
> ***"employee" in a traditional job?***

Even with the hard-knocks I'd taken, the answer was obvious: Working for myself in network marketing was the hands-down winner. No question.

Yes, I'd taken a few hits along the way, but bad things happen to people in all professions: people get laid-off, people get fired, products stop selling, companies close.

Welcome to life.

Taking Responsibility for My Results

I also came to another realization, which was my part in the process. Instead of blaming network marketing for my woes, I looked in the mirror and said, *"I'm to blame for what happened. I could have done my homework better. After all, who picked the companies I went to work for? It was me—I did. It was my poor judgment and my lack of experience that caused me a lot of the trouble I experienced."*

Now, looking back in retrospect, I am actually grateful for the adversity I went through. Sure, I stepped on a land mine or two (or six) along the way, but every experience—both the positive and the not so positive—has helped me become who I am today.

Choosing a Network Marketing Company

The series of negative experiences I had on what seemed like a roller coaster ride, with ups and downs that would never end, had one positive: It made me never want to go through those experiences again!

Eventually, after several false starts, I found the company I am still with to this day. What helped me move forward was taking the time to develop four specific criteria to consider when choosing a company in the future. In retrospect, I think the criteria I established for myself are what everyone entering the profession should consider. This is especially important if your goal is to establish a solid business that will provide you with decades of residual income.

I call it the Four Wheels Review, as if looking at the four wheels on a car:

Wheel #1: People

The first criteria for choosing a network marketing opportunity are the people behind the company.

- *"Who are the owners/founders of the organization?"*
- *What is their background?*
- *Have the founders been in network marketing before?*
- *If so, were they successful?*
- *Have they ever been sued?*
- *What happened to the previous company they founded?*
- *Did any of their distributors end up not being paid?*

Do your homework! Don't merely take the word of the person who's recruiting you. This individual may not have done his or her due diligence and is simply repeating what he or she has been told. (And if this person *did* discover negative information, he or she may choose not to share it with you, or just flat-out decide to lie.)

Wheel #2: Product

The second criteria for choosing the right opportunity is the product/product line).

- *Are the products "must-have" items, things that people already spend money on?*

- *Are the products "consumables" that need to be replaced every month (for example, toothpaste, vitamins, cosmetics etc.)?*

- *Are the products unique/branded to that one company, or are they nothing more than interchangeable "commodities" that can be bought anywhere?*

- *Are any of their products patented?*

The type of product/products you will be selling are critical to your success. Your ability to create loyal repeat customers will allow you to achieve consistent residual income.

If the products can be found at most other network marketing companies—*or worse, at major retailers like GNC, especially if they're sold at lower prices*—it's going to be hard to grow an income and almost impossible to create long-lasting residual income.

And you must make sure to Google the products to find out if the FDA has served any letters of violation. If so, check out what those violations are.

I was surprised to look at one company that was growing very well only to see that they were inspected by the FDA, and their products were determined to contain contaminants and even certain ingredients deemed dangerous to people's health.

Wheel #3: Compensation Plan

The third criteria for choosing a network marketing company is the compensation plan.

- *Is the compensation plan one that has proven successful over many decades?*

- *Does the compensation plan benefit everyone, or has it been specifically designed to benefit the company and/or a few top leaders over the majority of people?*

The problem for most people is it's hard to tell until it's too late. Make sure you go to the company website and learn what the plan is and how it works. Google "Income disclosure" and look at each rank position and what the annual or monthly income is per rank position. If the company doesn't provide this, it should serve as a red flag.

Wheel #4: Team

The fourth and final criteria for choosing a network marketing opportunity is the team you will be joining.

- *Is the team progressive, or do they have a traditional mindset approach to network marketing?*

- *Do the top leaders in your upline have experience in corporate management? For example, do they believe everything has to be done face to face and you have to go to meetings?*

Don't get me wrong. There's nothing wrong with doing meetings or home presentations, but if meetings/home parties are required to sell products and prospect/sponsor people, the time-intensiveness involved might be problematic.

Keep in mind that, in today's world, people's lives are very complicated. If your system for prospecting and sponsoring complicates their lives even more, they may start with you, but they probably won't stay. Adding people to your team is important, but if you don't keep them, you're just spinning your wheels.

Your job is to show people that your system brings quality and financial improvement to their life while increasing their time to enjoy it, not that it decreases or degrades all this. So if the team is progressive (for example, they teach effective ways to recruit via social media, and they have an online system/tools that support you in their Facebook groups), that's a good indication they are going to be a good fit.

But we're not done.

When it comes to the team you're joining and if you haven't decided on a sponsor, or if someone is trying to sponsor you, it's important to ask the following:

- *Has the person who is trying to prospect you kept his/her word when it comes to showing up on time and keeping appointments?*

- *Does he/she have any leaders you can talk to about their working relationship?*

- *Does this person only message with you or does he/she actually talk with you?*

- *Will this person do three-way calls or three-way zoom calls with you to your prospects?*

To be clear, you're not looking for your sponsor to build your business for you, but you *are* looking for someone who will train and support you until you can get established.

In summary: Just like a car that needs four wheels, I found that these four areas are vital for long-term network marketing success. If any of the four wheels are missing, you can't move forward. But when all four wheels are on the vehicle of your opportunity, you'll not only roll forward, you can race.

"Mountains are only a problem when they are bigger than you. Develop yourself so much that you become bigger than the mountains you face."

— *Idowu Koyenikan*

PART FIVE:

Passport to My Future

So now that I not only had a stable income, but one that was also rapidly growing, I was able to resume my happy life in Camden.

Every day I would go to this special place, somewhere a specific battle had taken place during the Revolutionary War. A large pond was spread out there, and I would spend my mornings reading, thinking and praying.

Then my father died.

I went back home and rented a house on a lake near my mom, the water providing me some of the same serenity I'd gotten used to at the pond back home, and I would go out on my jet ski several times each day.

The good thing was, at that time, I didn't need to work my business very hard. I'd sponsored 72 people directly. Out of those 72 people, three took it seriously. And for the next 20 years, the vast majority of my income would come from the teams I helped those three people build.

I Wanted to Go Places

One day, my company announced it was registering products in South Korea, which was great since I'd always been interested in Asia and Asian culture. The only problem was, I had a fear of traveling.

My main issue with going to Asia was I thought I needed to know the language. And, when it came to the idea of building a business there, I felt I needed know a lot about a country and its history.

I had a small team in Japan that had taken off well, but the top leader was really not good for that team. I could have gone over there and saved that team, but my fear of being in a foreign country held me back. I didn't go, and the team suffered.

I learned a lesson from that and decided I was never going to let fear hold me back ever again. So I went on the hunt to see if I could find a prospect in South Korea.

One of my networking friends gave me the name and email address of a doctor in Seoul, Korea. I emailed him and asked him to take a look at our company and product. I also asked him to consider my proven ability to lead a team. That night, he wrote me back. I was at a party at the time when I read his message. The message said:

> *Dear Mr. Altgilbers: If you want to do business with me, you need to come to Seoul, Korea, and you need to come now.*

I knew if I wanted to grow, both personally and pro-fessionally, I'd need to find the courage to do things I'd never done before and go places I'd never been before. Until that moment, my confidence had been limited by my past experiences. To get to the next level, I had to be willing to venture into the unknown.

I had a passport, but I'd never used it. So, why did I get it? I guess because I thought having one made me look cool. The fact that I'd taken the time to get the passport but had never used it was proof of two things:

- *I wanted to go places.*
- *I'd been too scared to do it.*

I decided on the spot that those days were over. Being scared and playing small hadn't served me. I put down my phone, turned to everyone at the party and said, *"Hey, guess what? I'm leaving for South Korea in the morning."*

Immediate Action Was Required

I realized I could not hesitate or my fears would set in again and paralyze me. So I moved fast. The following morning I drove to the airport in Columbia, S.C. and boarded a plane.

Twenty-four hours later, I landed in Seoul, South Korea.

The long flight left me dehydrated, and my legs were cramped. I came off the plane limping and exhausted. And, of course, no one around me spoke English. I was finally able to find a taxicab and told the driver the name of the hotel where I would be staying. The taxi driver nodded and off we sped.

A few minutes after we left the airport, the taxi passed through a military checkpoint. On one side stood Korean soldiers holding high-powered weapons, and on the other side were American soldiers holding high-powered weapons, too. *"This is crazy!"* I thought to myself. *"How in the hell am I going to build a business here when all everyone has on their mind is war?"*

Finally, we arrived at the hotel, where I met the man who'd agreed to meet with me. His name was John Huang, and I quickly learned was very serious about making money. He wanted to get into business right away.

I also discovered it wasn't just John who was interested in getting into business. Many Koreans were eager to make money. As tempted as I was to rush into getting him signed up and start training him, I told him it was important for the two of us to get to know each other.

I told John, *"Let's go out tonight and have drinks and dinner. Let's talk a bit and get to know each other."* He agreed. As it turned out, this going to dinner and getting to know each other before rushing into business was one of the best decisions I ever made.

Becoming Friends and Working Hard

Fortunately for both of us, John spoke English pretty well. It didn't take long for us to become good friends. And for the next 30 days, John and I drove his Audi all over South Korea, doing meetings in a number of cities.

Traveling around South Korea, I found myself experiencing a crash-course in the Korean culture. I also found myself deeply involved in doing the work, displaying a work ethic I had forgotten I was capable of. Our days would start early, and we would finish late at night. It had been years since I worked so hard, and it reminded me of my first 90 days, going from *eight to faint.*

The hard work John and I were doing together, each of us helping to build the other's business and future, helped us forge a friendship I do not feel could have been achieved any other way. *This* is one of the things I've come to appreciate most about network marketing.

Spending Time in Guam

John took me to the island of Guam, which was about a three-hour flight from Seoul. It was an American territory, and it used American money, with malls and franchise restaurants that were familiar to me. Most importantly, it was such a beautiful Pacific island, I immediately felt comfortable there.

In the third grade I'd drawn a crayon picture of myself on a boat, sailing to an island surround by a sea of bright blue-colored water. In my imagination, as a kid, I told myself a story about how, someday, I would live on that island. Now, I found myself standing on the sandy shore of an island, gazing at the Pacific Ocean, and I knew it was going to be my home.

I decided it was time to take my life and my business to a new level, not merely to travel this time but to settle down.

Leaving the United States

After my month-long trip to South Korea with John Haung, I flew back to the United States, sold my dream home, boxed up what was important, and shipped it to the island of Guam. Then I flew back and leased a penthouse on the beach.

To wake up every day to the sound of the ocean was amazing.

Where I lived was quiet and remote. Often, when I would go down to the beach, I found myself alone. Just me and the Pacific Ocean, standing on white sand, gazing out at blue water, just like in the picture I had drawn as a kid.

Using Guam as my base, I worked at building my business throughout Korea, traveling to Seoul, South Korea, on a regular basis.

Seoul is a big city, as big as New York City—very clean, safe, and sophisticated—and with mountains! I would often go hiking in the mountains just outside the city, sometimes with the leaders on my team. I quickly fell in love with these people and their culture.

This was a major turning point in my life, to experience something so unexpectedly wonderful outside of the United States. Clearly, I never would have known any of it had I not been willing to take a leap of faith and travel there.

The Asian Work Ethic

While engaging with the leaders on my team, I discovered the strong work ethic of the Korean people. In the United States people worked to live, but the Korean people lived to work.

Now, I'm not saying one way is better than the other. There's a lot to be said for the benefits of life-balance. I work hard, but I also believe in relaxing and enjoying life.

It seemed like the Koreans had one gear, and that gear was working hard. This made building a team there a joy. As a result, I soon found myself with a bigger vision for my business, one that included more of Asia.

Expanding My Business Footprint

Since Asia is made up of many countries, I put the word out to my leaders back in the United States and asked: *"Who do you know in Asia? Use me while I'm here!"*

This technique, called "tap-rooting" (working through leaders to find other leaders, which I will talk about a little later) was something I was aware of but had never done.

After telling my leaders back in the states that I'd go anywhere in Asia for them, I had a leader by the name of Teri Shuler reach out and ask me if I would go to the Philippines. She had some people there whom she thought would be interested in the opportunity.

I flew to Manila, and my first night I found 50 hungry people in the room, almost all of them ready to get started. Soon I found myself working in South Korea *and* the Philippines.

Shortly thereafter, I decided to open a temporary office in Manila. Teri was willing to come live there and run that office.

Eventually, over a period of time, that country was doing millions of dollars of sales. For the past 15 years, it continues to be a great market.

Working Your Available Assets

When it comes to building a business, it's smart to tap into every contact you have at the present time. I say this because many people sign someone up, get them started, and assume they'll work every possible angle to build their business.

They won't.

I realized if I wanted to grow my business, it was up to *me* to help people see the possibilities around them—even if it means helping people add members to their team who don't immediately make you money. It's up to *you* to call your leaders and start picking their minds and ask them, *"Who do you know?"*

I did that with one of my leaders in Canada. Her name was Linda Emmerson, and she had not done much with the business. So I called her and said, *"Linda, you've been in network marketing companies before. Who do you know in Asia?"*

She said, *"I know a woman in Singapore, but I already talked to her about this, and she's not interested."*

Most people would have taken her at her word, that the person wasn't interested. But I knew Linda wasn't strong enough yet in terms of her skills. I was. So I said, *"Okay, why not give me her phone number anyway?"*

The woman's name was Sheri, and I called her. She agreed to a lunch appointment, so I flew to Singapore. *Yes, I flew to Singapore to meet with someone I'd been told wasn't interested.* Sheri agreed to join, and I sponsored her right *under*

Linda—not under me, but under Linda, since Linda was the person who'd given me the lead.

Sheri's team eventually began producing $2 million per month in sales. Was it worth flying to Singapore? I don't know, you tell me.

Never, Ever Assume

I asked that same *"Who do you know?"* question of a leader in Hawaii. She was Japanese, had been in several network marketing companies before and had moderate success. She told me she knew someone in Tokyo, but he was already successful, so she knew he wouldn't be interested.

I learned long ago to never to buy into people's *"red light stories"* by assuming they're correct in their assessments of a situation or a prospect's level of desire.

I said, *"Well, I like to talk to successful people. If he says no, that's fine, but let me talk to him."*

Here's what's interesting: Even with nothing to lose, with me offering to make the call, she proceeded to create *another* roadblock! *"He doesn't speak English, and you don't speak Japanese, so I don't see how you're going to be able to talk to him."*

"You're right," I said. *"But you speak Japanese and English, right? Well, I have this feature in my phone called a three-way call, so how about letting me call him, and then I can connect the three of us together, and you can translate. Would you be willing to do that?"*

She reluctantly said yes.

An hour later the man who I'd just been told wouldn't join because he was already successful joined *her* team, with *my* help. Today, that man has a very large team in Japan, and we all made money. Assuming the man wouldn't be interested would have been very expensive for all of us.

It's not your job to say "no" for other people. If someone wants to say no, let them. But never do it for them.

Never assume.

"In the end, you won't remember the time you spent working in the office or mowing your lawn. Climb that damn mountain!"

— *Jack Kerouac*

PART SIX:

China

As I continued to tap-root for prospects in Asia by working my team for leads back in the U.S., our company made a major announcement: It was opening up Taiwan to distributors. Being in Guam, I lived so close to Taiwan, it made sense for to me to try.

The only problem, of course, was I didn't know anybody there—not to mention I could neither read nor speak a word of Mandarin Chinese. But, armed with a new level of courage from my recent successes in Japan and South Korea, I decided to go.

And the sooner the better. After all, if the early bird gets the worm, why not be the earliest bird of all? So I rushed to the airport, got on the plane, and touched down in Taiwan just three hours after the announcement had been made.

After I got off the plane, I took a taxi into Taipei, still wondering what my next move would be and how I might find anybody to join me. While I had no concrete plan, I believed in the power of asking proactive, empowering questions. So I kept repeating to myself, *"What's my next move?"*

Every time that little negative voice in my head said, *"This will never work!"* I replaced it with, *"What's my next move?"*

When no answer arrived, I walked out to the street and hailed a taxi. When I climbed in, the taxi driver asked me, *"Where are you going?"* I didn't have an answer for him. The only thing I knew for sure was the answer wasn't back at the hotel.

And then it hit me.

Though the company I was with wasn't active yet, I knew of another company who had a large presence in Taiwan. I told the taxi driver to take me there. If nothing else, I could see what their offices and distribution support center looked like.

Asking for Help

When I arrived at the company's office, admiring the marble floors and exquisite décor, I found a group of Chinese leaders enthusiastically making a presentation to a group of prospects. The pace was frenetic, like watching bees in a beehive.

People looked at me curiously, and one of the men got up and approached me. He spoke English and asked me, *"Are you my Blue Diamond from America?"*

I replied, *"No, I'm just a tourist. I just arrived here in Taiwan for the first time, and I've always admired your company. I wanted to see what the operation looked like."* Then I asked, *"Is there a network marketing magazine that's published in Taiwan that network marketers read?"*

He said there was.

I asked him if he would be willing to help me by taking me there, so I could meet the publisher. *"And I would like to take you to lunch,"* I said. Without hesitation, the man said yes.

Five minutes later, the man and I were in the taxi on the way to the magazine's offices.

When People Keep Saying "Yes"...

As we were driving, I asked the man if we could stop somewhere that I could buy a cell phone with a local number, and he agreed to help me with that, too.

After meeting with the magazine publisher, who (fortunately) also spoke English, I placed an ad using the phone number of the new phone I'd just purchased.

Next, I asked the man if he would mind helping me get a studio apartment.

He agreed to help me do that.

Then I asked him if he could help me get a small office that I could rent.

Again, he said yes.

Then I asked him if he could translate simple brochures for me and help me with my presentations.

Again, he said yes.

Then I asked him if he'd be willing to help me translate my live presentations to prospects. *"I'd be willing to pay you for your time,"* I said.

Again, he said yes.

I learned three important lessons that day:

1. *If an opportunity presents itself, don't hesitate—jump on it.*

2. *If you need help, sometimes all you've got to do is ask.*

And...

3. *When someone keeps telling you "yes," don't stop.*

Just keep asking.

Who Else Do You Know?

Before long, interested people from all over Taiwan started calling me. I hopped subways, taxicabs and trains. I flew to different parts of the island—which was amazing since I'd started off not knowing a single person.

As I met different people in my travels in Asia, I would always ask for referrals. I sounded like a broken record, asking every person over and over again: *"Who else do you know?"* It became like a mantra. And when my company announced they were going to open Thailand, I put the word out to everyone I knew: *"Who knows anyone in Thailand?"*

One day I asked someone the *"Who else do you know?"* question and received a referral. I called the person immediately, and the guy agreed to meet me at the airport in Bangkok. When we met, it didn't take long for us to see that we would make a great team.

My new leader and I collaborated, doing meetings all over the country in Thailand and building the business. I was there so much, I decided to get a condo in Bangkok.

The Speed of the Leader

I imagine many people who hear my story will find themselves wondering why I always went so hard and fast. Part of it is my nature. Another part is my fear that if I don't go hard and fast, I may not go at all.

The main reason, however, is my belief that *the speed of the team is the speed of the leader*.

Imagine you wanted to go from Bar Harbor, Maine to San Diego. Well, you can walk, but how long would it take you to walk 3,260 miles? Walking 10 miles a day, it would take you almost a year. That's just too long. So why not run? If you run, you could cut the time in half, right? Then again...

- *Why run when you can ride a bike and get there in a month?*

- *Why ride a bike when you can take a car and get there in five days?*

- *Why drive a car when you can take a plane and get there in five hours?*

Then again, why take a plane when you can take a rocket ship?

My point is this: The distance between where you are now and where you want to be is the same distance! The only question is how long it's going to take you to move from point A to point B. The only difference isn't the distance, it's the *speed*.

Momentum Matters

From my experience, the speed of the leader sets the pace for the rest of the pack. If you're slow, they're slow. If you're nonchalant, they're nonchalant. If you have a sense of urgency with a *"hit the floor running"* mindset, your people will, too.

I believe massive action creates massive results. I also believe to build slow is torture. I wanted to build with speed and just get it done. When I got going in network marketing, I said to myself, I want to get it done.

Don't get me wrong: There are many ways to work this business, and there's nothing that says you have to work it the way I do. That's the amazing thing about network marketing, you get to do it *your* way. But don't underestimate the impact momentum has on other people.

Momentum matters.

(That's the beauty of a "90-Day 'Quick Climb' Plan" which you'll find later in this book. It's an all-out massive action plan that builds momentum—so if you're game, buckle up!)

When You're Close, Don't Quit!

One time, I was working with a very driven women in Singapore named Sheri Din (who I mentioned earlier).

For Sheri, becoming a success wasn't about money, it was about the recognition. She believed (rightly so) that women in her culture could be every bit as successful as men could. And, while I do not in any way think of myself as sexist, I'd assumed the top leader in Singapore would be a man.

Sheri was about to become number-one, and she was ready to prove everyone wrong.

One night, I was in a piano lounge in Taipei with some of the leaders there. Sheri called me from Malaysia, and she was crying, which was very unlike her. It was too loud in the lounge to hear her, so I exited the lounge and found myself standing in the pouring rain, my phone pressed to my ear.

"What is it? What's wrong?" I asked.

Sheri got control of herself and told me why she was so upset. There were only a few days left in the month, and she was just short of reaching what would have made her the first person to reach the highest rank in Singapore and Malaysia.

I said, *"Okay, we've got a few days left, right? Let's run! Who do I need to talk to? What can we do? Let's do it!"*

For the next 72 hours, Sheri and I got busy and stayed focused on her goal. She pushed and pushed and pushed. There was no quit in her.

And she made it.

The Right Type of Personality

During my time working in Asia I had the opportunity to work with many different kinds of people, with wildly different personalities. Sheri, who was as driven a person as I'd ever met, was a good example. Others, who were nowhere as driven as Sheri, did well, also.

Which leads to a very important question:

Are there personality types that are more likely to succeed than others?

It's an interesting question indeed.

Generally speaking, people tend to be in one of two personality groups: *introverts* and *extroverts*.

Introverts (as you probably already know), tend to be shy and reserved. Extroverts, on the other hand, are people who we think of as being more out-going and sociable, people who often stand out in a crowd. The fact is:

- *Some people are methodical and detail oriented, others aren't.*

- *Some people are spontaneous and impulsive, others take forever to make decisions and get started.*

- *Some people are extremely competitive and want to win at all costs, while others are happy with only a moderate level of success.*

So which is best suited for network marketing? Beats me. I'm reluctant to give an answer because during my 40 years in the profession, I've seen both types be successful. And I've seen both types fail. I've learned to never judge people based on how well I think they're going to do.

Never Prejudge People, Ever

I believe it's impossible to determine which personality types are best suited for network marketing. And even if it's possible, I think it's stupid and unfair—stupid to eliminate potential future leaders on your team using potentially-flawed criteria and unfair to the person you're prospecting.

If you want to build a successful team, my best advice is that you should never, ever prejudge someone. And this is particularly important in regard to whether you think someone might be a customer for your product and/or whether you think they may be potential member of your team.

Never, *ever* prejudge.

Making decisions for other people is not your job. The only way to determine if someone might be successful in this profession is to offer them the opportunity and let *them* determine if it's right for them.

People Can and Do Change

Over the years I've heard it said that people's personalities are inherited, the result of genetics—and that they don't change. This is something I have come to know is simply not true.

People's personalities can be (and often are) shaped and influenced by their experiences and their environment.

People can and do change.

This is another reason you should never prejudge someone when it comes to their perceived chances of being successful in this business. A person may not have what it takes to succeed when they start, but that may well change once they get involved. I've seen many such transformations take place before my very eyes.

"There's no glory in climbing a mountain if all you want to do is to get to the top. It's experiencing the climb itself— in all its moments of revelation, heartbreak, and fatigue—that has to be the goal."

– Karyn Kusama

PART SEVEN:

Music, Michelle and Social Media

One of the central loves of my life has always been music. *I love it.* Ironically, it was music that brought me into the orbit of one of my other great loves—my wife, Michelle. And my family.

My love of music started when I was in eighth grade. One day, I went over to see a friend who played guitar. And on this particular day, another friend was there—someone who also played guitar. I sat there, listening to them play a song by Creedence Clearwater Revival (a big band at the time) and being impressed at how good they were. Truth be told, I was also a bit jealous.

Suddenly, his mother walked up and handed me a microphone, then she gave me a piece of paper with the lyrics to the song. *"Here, sing with them,"* she said. I did, and to everyone's surprise (including mine), I was pretty good.

That simple action by an adult who could see I wanted to join in was a turning point for me.

From that moment, I was hooked.

I became a lead singer in various bands, eventually learning to play the drums, too. One moment I'm in the eighth grade, watching other people play music—four years later I'm the lead singer/drummer in a rock band.

Go figure.

Music Was Pushed Aside

However, after I got out of high school—trying to decide what I was going to do with my life—my musical career got pushed aside. Music just wasn't paying the bills.

Like so many people, I turned my attention to the task of making a living. While my love of music never went away, I just didn't have the time to pursue it.

Fortunately, when I got involved in network marketing in Taiwan, I discovered there were a lot of piano bars. One place I used to frequent was a very classy piano bar, where people could get up and sing—kind of like karaoke, but with a live band—and with brilliant musicians.

I went there every chance I could.

Over time, I got to know the owner of the piano bar. His name was Vince, and he'd have different musicians come in and sing or play the piano. And from time to time, Vince would invite me to get up and sing. It was a blast.

And it's how I met my wife.

Meeting Michelle

One night I was at Vince's piano bar, and a young woman came through the door. Her name was Michelle. She was very beautiful, and boy, could she sing!

I introduced myself to her.

Not long after, I went to the piano bar late one night, and Michelle came again. I sat there watching, enthralled, as she sang a number by Nat King Cole. Michelle put her heart and soul into the music, like she owned not just the stage but the entire room.

When she was done, I went up to her and asked, *"Do you know what you're singing about?"*

She said, *"No."*

I said, *"Well, you sure sound like you do."*

A few minutes later, she came up to me and asked if I wanted to sing a song with her. I said, *"Well, I don't know. What do you have?"*

Michelle showed me some of her sheet music, and we picked a song. She started playing the piano, and I started singing. That's how it happened.

One year later we got married on the island of Guam.

Back to the States

After Michelle became pregnant with our son, Arthur (Michelle also had a son named Alexander), I asked her if she would be willing to live in the United States. I told her, *"When we get there, we'll buy a house with big windows that will look out over the Great Smoky Mountains. I'll buy you a piano and put it right in the window, and you can look out and play."*

She agreed, and it wasn't long before we were on a plane headed to the United States.

When we got to America, we went to Gatlinburg, located in the heart of Great Smoky Mountains National Park, and searched for properties. After a month of looking, we found what we were searching for—a spectacular 4,500-square-foot house with an open floor plan and high, vaulted ceilings.

And big windows.

After we bought the house (which, because of my years in network marketing, we were able to pay for in *cash*), I made good on my other promise and bought Michelle a piano (a Steinway, Model D, the biggest piano Steinway makes) which we put right in the window, overlooking the mountains below.

Network marketing had not only changed me financially, it had given me a quality and aspect of the life I had always been missing—one that included a family.

Now I had that, too.

Mountain Versus Island Living

My life had changed in a big way. I was no longer hopping taxi cabs, planes and trains across Asia. Before, my goals were to be successful in network marketing. Now, I set out to be a professional husband and father to my wife and children.

And that's what I did.

For the next five years, I focused exclusively on my family and remodeling our home. I was truly living the dream that so many people want, with a great family and financially free enough to spend time enjoying the things that are most important.

After getting the family settled, including tasks like figuring out which schools the boys would attend, I hired some skilled carpenters to renovate the house, adding 6,500 square feet of interior space to the house and a 5,000-square-foot exterior deck (which was also paid for in cash).

Ours was a family with no debt.

Pursuing My Other Dream

After we moved in, music continued to be a central part of our lives—and it continues to be part of it to this day. Michelle spends much of her time singing and playing. Alexander, our 17-year old, is very skilled on the piano, too. And Arthur, who is 10, is getting very good as well.

But there was something else that I wanted to do, and that was to explore my potential as a musician, singer and song writer. I had been a drummer and vocalist in bands when I was young, and I would hear songs in my head—songs I couldn't play on a piano or guitar.

During my time in the Philippines, I'd had the good fortune to meet many really great musicians. One of these people was a music director and skilled guitarist, Jun Tamayo. I told Jun I had written a lot of song lyrics, but I didn't play guitar or piano, and asked if he'd be willing to help me.

Jun said, *"No problem. Let's go into the studio."*

That began a relationship that continued for over a decade, resulting in 4 CDs of original songs, which are actually on iTunes today. I laughed when I started getting residual income from my music, though the income from my music is nowhere near as large as it is from network marketing!

The Times, They Were a Changin'

After being absent from network marketing for almost six years, I realized the profession was changing. Social media was beginning to bloom, and it was affecting all areas of our lives and business, whether we liked it or not. Online tools and methods were becoming the preferred choice over personal interaction. I had not even seen one of my company's distributor kits in six years, so I decided to order one.

When the distributor kit arrived, I looked at it and shook my head. *"This is how they still teach the business?"* I wondered. The kit promoted the traditional methods of doing home parties. I knew there had to be a better way. The modern world was turning to smart phones, using online strategies, and tapping highly entrepreneurial methods.

The problem with many people who have been in network marketing for a long time is they quit learning. They go into what I call a "success coma." They always assume that the income they're getting every month will always remain the same (or get better) and, when it doesn't, they think they simply need to work harder with the same methods they used before.

Then, when they don't get the results that they use to get, they become critical of their downline or just assume people are not interested in network marketing anymore.

That is a mistake.

Time never changes the fundamentals of the business, but it always has an effect on the tools and methods with which the business is communicated and built.

Finding Help From People Who Know

I decided to seek out people who could help and mentor me, and I didn't want it to be someone my age. As a baby boomer (defined as a person born between 1946-1964), I felt it was critical to seek the guidance of people who were good at seeing the world through the eyes of those in Generation Y and Z.

So after getting some good advice, I created a 10-minute video presentation and other tools that could be emailed to anyone in the world on how to do the business. Then I sought out professional coaching through someone who was highly regarded in the skills needed to be successful in today's world of social media-based network marketing. That person was Ray Higdon (which is why I asked him to write the foreword to this book).

Ray got me clear on what social media is, how it works, and why it's so important to do it right.

As Ray suggested, I started doing daily Facebook Live calls and building my social media following. Today, I have people all around the world who get on my Facebook Lives, watch my YouTube videos, and seek me out for coaching.

I knew that if others were to experience my level of success, I needed to know how to do it with today's tools, not just the tools and approaches I'd used in the past. The rearview mirror is great for reminiscing, not for business-building.

Don't get me wrong. In terms of relationship-building, I still believe there is nothing better than getting to meet with people in person, face to face. But the world moves on, and new tools exist.

So why not use them all?

"Each fresh peak ascended teaches something."

— *Sir Martin Convay*

PART EIGHT:

Other Things Worth Knowing

Sell the Franchise, Not the Hamburger

Early on, I learned something I have taught to others for years now, which is to *sell the franchise, not the hamburger*.

Most people are familiar with McDonalds, it's virtually impossible not to be. But not everyone knows the story *behind* McDonalds.

In 1954, Ray Kroc—who sold milkshake machines for a living—stepped into a small but extremely busy restaurant in San Bernardino, Calif. run by two brothers. What caught Ray's attention wasn't the food so much (which was tasty, but not gourmet by any means), it was the stunning effectiveness of the operation.

The system.

Unlike most restaurants, McDonald's offered a limited menu of just burgers, fries and beverages. As such, they were able to control the quality of the food consistently and serve it quickly to large numbers of customers.

Ray Kroc bought the exclusive rights to the McDonald's name and operating system because he understood the magic of what he was seeing. The McDonald brothers thought they were in the *food* business. Ray Kroc understood they were in the *systems* business. He saw a business model that could be *duplicated* and *franchised*.

As an interesting side note, Kroc promoted his efforts to sell franchises with the slogan, *"In business for yourself, but not by yourself."* (Sounds a lot like network marketing, doesn't it?)

Until that time, I'd been solely focused on selling the product (the *hamburger*). After that day in Nashville, I understood that if I was ever going to become wealthy, I needed to shift my efforts to selling people on the franchise (the *system*).

Sometimes people ask me, *"If you focus your attention on selling the business, who's consuming the product?"* My answer to that is, *"Did you ever know anyone to buy a franchise who didn't consume their own products?"*

Tap-Rooting Your Way to Success

One of the things I love is the rich vegetation we get living up in the Smokey Mountains of Tennessee. There are over 1,600 species of flowering plants.

So, what do plants have to do with network marketing? Well, one of your biggest keys to success is right here, so let me explain.

You see, plants have two kinds of root systems. One is a bunch of little roots (like hair almost) that go into the ground and feed the plant. The other, a taproot system, is one large, thick, central root that goes straight downward and all the other roots sprout from it.

What I highly recommend is something I call "tap-rooting" and if you think of yourself as that main root, you focus and work through all those smaller roots shooting off from you.

So, what does this look like?

Well, when you have a team that starts growing, you get to know the people down below. In other words, not just the people you personally sponsored. Start talking to them and get to know their background, where they've been in life, and who they've come to know. What kind of people do they know?

I went several levels down in my organization and found people who were playing average. And yet they had a goldmine of people they knew. I tapped into their mine because all I asked was, *"Who do you know that has been involved in a business similar to this one that you could introduce me to?"*

Sometimes they would tell me they already had talked to the person and the person was not interested. And I would say I understood but inside I was thinking, they haven't met me yet. So, I'd ask for the person's phone number, then sign them up under that person.

If you tap-root into your organization, like a beautiful, strong plant, you're going to grow.

Drive Deep Legs

I believe that your depth is your security, so I always work through my leaders. I am all about support, support, support. I'm not a "sponsor monster" who's going to throw mud against the wall and see what sticks. I think that's another definition of insanity.

If you look at the history of the top income earners in this network marketing world, you can go back to the very beginnings of this industry and see that most of their volume comes from one or two legs—and that's it. Even today, when I have people reach out or I talk to people, I don't sponsor direct to myself, I sponsor under the leaders—leaders I can really depend on, those who I know will take care of those new people.

People Talk Too Much

Some people just don't get the results they want from their presentations, then get frustrated and wonder what's going on. You might be surprised by what I'm going to say next. Well, it's not about what is being said. Nope. It's exactly the opposite.

Most people are talking too much!

What are they doing? They are trying to sell people. They're so hungry to get that person to join and so they try to win them over just talking, talking, talking. Somehow, if they talk them to death, the prospect will join.

Talking endlessly just gets the prospect (even if they're related to you or you are good friends) thinking to themselves, *"I'm so busy, I don't have time for this kind of thing, I'm not in sales."*

All because they are being "pitched" to. I see new people ruin their warm market that would be interested, nuking people with enthusiasm and too much talking.

What's the answer? Whatever you are presenting must be done in a very short timeframe, ideally within a few minutes. That's why a video is the best way to go because it's professionally produced so it's going to do the hard work and tell the prospect why this would be a solution to their problems, why you have an opportunity, and what this opportunity can do for them.

Then all you have to do is call them 30 minutes after you've sent that link and be in front of your computer and enroll them. And be casual, *"I really think this is something we both could do together and have a lot of fun and make some money. How do you feel—would you like to do that with me?"*

Make it fun, don't make it serious. Most people don't like serious. Their lives are already crazy and serious, so they don't want more of that, right?

If you call the prospect back and they try to get you to do the motormouth thing and didn't look at your video, don't violate the process. Stick to the plan.

Just laugh and say, *"Hey Janet, okay something happened, when I sent you that link..."* And she'll maybe say something about getting distracted by the kids, her husband or her work, and it's all handled now. With that, just get things right back on track.

"Okay, great, do you have 10 minutes (or whatever length your video is) *to watch it?"* If she says, *"Well, what is it again?"* Say, *"You know Janet, I think the video does a perfect job of really getting the message across and explaining everything. How about I'll call you back in, let's say, 20 minutes if you can look at it now—okay?"*

You let the tool do the work and focus on the follow-up. I followed this very principle, and it's not rocket science, there's nothing fancy about it. I was just dumb enough to do it! That's why educated people struggle with this stuff because there isn't anything to this.

Send the link, follow up, enroll the person, and don't be a motormouth. Talking too much ruins it every time.

Dealing With People's Emotions

Anyone who wants to be successful in this business must learn to deal with emotions—yours, of course, but just as important, the emotions of others.

I've worked with people in both my upline and my downline who are emotionally needy people. This manifests itself most often in people's need to be the center of attention.

I remember a guy who constantly talked about himself. It wasn't just me who noticed—*everyone did*. He talked about himself so often that someone suggested he read the book, "How to Win Friends and Influence People." He said he already had. So he was a know-it-all, too!

He's no longer with me.

I couldn't continue to be around him, let alone help him build his business. How much did this cost him? I don't know. There are a number of leaders on my team who earn mid-six-figure incomes. Can you imagine losing $25,000 every month simply because you needed to make yourself the center of attention?

In this business, our minds can't be on ourselves. Our minds must be on helping *others* fulfill *their* needs. As Zig Ziglar is famous as having said, *"You can get everything in life that you want if you'll just help enough other people get what they want."*

Feeling Unworthy

There's a scene in the movie "Wayne's World" where the two main characters, Wayne and Garth (played by actors Mike Meyers and Dana Carvey), get on their knees and chant, *"We're not worthy! We're not worthy!"* It's a funny scene.

But it's a sad reality for many people in the world of network marketing.

Feelings of unworthiness keep people from earning at the level they deserve probably more than any other factor. And even when people *do* start earning at a high level, I've watched them go broke. How is that possible? It's because they have the wrong self-image. They see themselves as unworthy of the money they're earning and then engage in acts of subconscious self-sabotage, making bad investments, drinking to excess, and/or spending on luxury items they really don't need.

I started in this business suffering with my own feelings of unworthiness, but I learned to deal with them. I did this primarily by reading positive books and listening to motivational audios.

If you want to be successful in this profession, you must explore your core beliefs, identify anything that you believe may be holding you back, and deal with them.

Working on yourself and your mindset is not a nice-to-do side project, it's a core essential.

Whenever Possible, Do Business in Person

I believe in building relationships. Last year, I spent three solid months traveling different Asian countries to meet with leaders to have lunch or dinner with them, not just doing training (though that's important, too) but simply bonding.

This is how you create a strong team that is going to last.

Online videos, social media and email are great timesavers, but there will never be a replacement for the relationship-building that comes with meeting people in person, having a glass of wine and breaking bread, or being engaged in some kind of team building activity.

Back in the 1980s, I would routinely spend a thousand dollars a month on phone bills. Seriously. And it could cost upward of $500 dollars just to do a conference call for 25 people! As a result, people were forced to keep things simple. Today, the cost for a 2,000-person conference call is near zero.

In those days, people were forced to talk to each other to learn what they wanted from the business. You looked people in the eye and asked them who they knew (which was the quickest way to get people into action).

The tools and technology are highly efficient today, but are they really more effective? Efficiency reduces work and increases speed. *Effectiveness is about results.* It's about doing what works, even if it costs a bit more or takes a bit longer. That's the great irony. Sometimes the easier something is, the harder it becomes.

Whenever possible, do the business in person.

Stay Focused and Committed

You can't win the Kentucky Derby riding two horses at once. You've got to make up your mind which one you're going to ride. In the same way, I've yet to find anybody who can build with two companies at the same time and be successful.

Maybe they're out there, but I've never met them.

One of the things I liked about network marketing 40 years ago was that people only knew about the one company they were involved with. They didn't spend time surfing around looking for other options, they just got to work.

Today there are so many that when you hold an opportunity meeting in a hotel, there are other opportunity meetings going on just down the hall. I'm not saying that having options is a problem—options are a good thing. But *too many options* can become a distraction. People spend time worrying about what everyone else is doing. If they'd just spent that time putting their nose down and getting to work, they'd already have been on their way to building a team.

Building a Prospecting List

Your prospect list is the foundation of your business. I still have every name and every phone number of every person on my prospect lists from 20 years ago. Always keep that list and keep adding to it over time.

Who goes on your list? Everyone you know and everyone with whom you come in contact. And never prejudge (I mentioned this earlier, but it can never be said often enough). Never decide for other people if your opportunity is right for them or not. *That is not your job.* Your job is simply to put their names and phone numbers down on your prospect list.

It's easy to think someone might not be interested because they make a lot of money and are doing well. Or because they're doctors or lawyers, they won't have the time to look at the business, let alone do it.

I've found the exact opposite to be true. The irony is, the busier people are, the more productive they tend to be. They know how to multitask and get things done.

Prospecting Strangers

When you're out shopping, standing at a long line somewhere like Starbucks, instead of looking at your phones, why not use that time to start a conversation with the person next to you?

This idea may be foreign—even shocking, perhaps—to some of you. (Jeff, did you just suggest I talk to a human? Yes, I did.)

This is another skill set people in my generation had, one that is lost on younger people.

The great thing is, the skill of starting a conversation with a stranger, *combined* with the convenience of cell phones, is very powerful. Once a connection has been made, you can say, *"You know, I really enjoyed our conversation. Do you use Facebook?"*

Inviting People

I see lots of people jump right into the presentation, either with their product or with their opportunity. This is a mistake. They're missing *the invitation* part of the process.

The invitation is just what it sounds like: It's an *invitation* to hear a presentation, not the presentation itself.

The best part is, you don't have to be an expert to invite someone to hear about an opportunity any more than you need to be an expert at inviting someone to a party. You just invite them.

Many people coming into network marketing worry about having to be good at sales. It's one of the reasons they refuse to get involved in the business. That's why the invitation is so important, because their first contact with the business isn't being sold anything. They were simply invited to listen.

Selling is a difficult skill for many people. Inviting someone to consider an opportunity is something anyone can master.

Let me give you an example of how to share an invitation call. You say, *"Hey, I'm glad I caught you. Listen, I found something I'm excited about, something we both can do together and have a lot of fun and make a lot of money. Have you got 10 minutes to look at it? I think it's something you'd be great at."*

Point is, keep it fun and whatever you do, don't make it overly serious. Nobody is interested in anything that sounds serious. They'll say yes or no. In any case, you've done your job.

Never Summarize the Opportunity!

When people ask, *"What's this about?"* it's tempting to jump in and start summarizing the opportunity.

Don't.

Hundreds of thousands of research dollars go into the creation of those videos—the information on them, the order in which that information is presented, and the visuals that enhance and support the audio.

Make no mistake—no matter how good you are, 99 out of 100 times, a summary will only lead to a no. Summarizing a 15- or 20-minute video in five minutes in an attempt to save time is *never* more effective than having a prospect watch the entire thing themselves.

Three Levels of Success in Network Marketing

There are three levels people go through in this business (and, for that matter, any business). And each of the three start with the letter "S"...

- **Sustenance:** This is the level where you are able to pay your bills and make a living.

- **Success:** This is the level where you can afford the nicer things in life, like your dream house (as opposed to simply having a roof over your head).

- **Significance:** This is the final (and ultimate) level where you find *meaning* and *purpose* beyond material things—where contributing to others and becoming a "servant leader" become the priorities.

The first two levels can be achieved through training, discipline and persistence. The final level, however—*significance*—requires something more. It requires that you focus on others in a way that is designed to benefit them, even if it never benefits you.

That's true significance.

"If you find a man or woman standing at the top of a mountain, it's a pretty safe bet they didn't just fall there."

— Anonymous

PART NINE:

The 90-Day "Quick Climb" Plan

For me, there's been nothing more effective in terms of getting results than having a strong 90-day plan. I believe this is true no matter how long you've been in this business—40 years (like me) or only four days. Because if you want to make things happen and get your business off the ground, you've got to create some momentum.

That's the 90-Day 'Quick Climb' Plan.

The 90-Day Plan

I look at my 90-day plan in the same way NASA looks at a space shuttle launch. When the shuttle takes off, it's got 2 million pounds of fuel. That's what it needs just to escape the gravity of our atmosphere to get into space.

In the same way, when I joined my current network marketing company (which I've been in for the past 20 years), I knew that massive residual income wasn't going to happen without an initial burst of massive action.

You must have a burst of energy—of all out, massive action—and really go for it. You put out like you've never put out before.

Using an all-out, 90-day plan, I put 800 members on my team. And, by the way, I did it without leaving my driveway and without doing a single meeting. I didn't even own a computer yet!

Here's the deal: The thing you need to know is, there are basics that never change. *Achieving success isn't about the tools.* Everybody seems to think that the *tools* are the key to building their business. No, it's not the tools. Tools help, but having tools doesn't make it happen. It's all out, massive action—that's what makes it happen. Your commitment to the success of your business, combined with massive action, that's the key.

Principles of the 90-Day Plan

So, what's involved in the 90-day plan? Before we get into the framework, let's start with the foundation. There are Five Principles you need to understand before you begin.

The 1st Principle: Definition

The first principle in terms of having a successful 90-day plan is to define exactly what you're trying to achieve.

- *Is it a new rank?*

- *More income?*

- *Adding a certain number of people in your downline?*

- *Achieving team sales volume goals?*

Maybe you're one of those leaders who's been dancing in the shadows all these years. Well, it's time to get out of the shadows!

Define—in print—*exactly* what your 90-day goals are going to be. What it is that you *really* want to achieve. For example, when I did my 90-day plan, I had one goal in mind: *my goal was to create a personal income of $5,000 a month.*

That's all I thought about the entire 90 days. I thought, "If I could get my income to $5,000 per month, I could pay my bills and support my family. In my third month, my check was over five thousand dollars. That was my *singular* 90-day goal, and I reached it because that was *all* I focused on.

The 2nd Principle: Clarity

I know what you're thinking: Isn't that what we just did in the first principle? Get clear on the goal? Well, that's not the clarity I'm talking about.

I'm talking about creating clarity with everyone around you.

You want to let everyone in your life—family, friends, team members—know precisely what you're doing, what you're trying to achieve. If you're married, you need to discuss this with your spouse because you're not going to have a lot of time for the family. You're going to be 100 percent focused on the mission you defined, so you need to make sure that your spouse and other members of your family are on board.

Sit your family down and say, *"Listen, I'm going to commit to something—something I haven't done before—and I really need everyone's support. It means that I won't be available very often to do family things. Sometimes, I might not be available at all."*

It's not enough for you to commit to your 90-day plan: Everyone in the family needs to be onboard and actively support your goal. And make sure everyone knows that what you're doing is for the benefit of the entire family. That's why you need their help. You're not just doing it for yourself, you're also doing it for *them*.

This is what I told my family. And it was entirely true! My family is still living on the income from the team I built during that 90-day period. Let that sink in for a minute. I did a 90-day run 20 years ago, and my family is still reaping the rewards.

The 3rd Principle: Permission

Permission is about collaboration. Since network marketing is based on collaboration, you'll want to involve your team in what you're doing. Since you're the leader, you have a group of people you have to get permission from.

What I mean by this is you want to get everyone on your team to sign on/buy into your plan. If you don't, you're bound to have trouble. No, it's worse than that. *If you don't get people to buy into playing their part in your 90-day plan, your plan will fail.* In fact, you won't even get through the first 30 days.

The main reason for this is that your people are not all the same. Some are full-time, some part-time, others less than that. Some are committed to their own success, others aren't. Some have lots of time to dedicate to the business, others don't.

So, what can you do?

The answer is to set individual goals for each person on your team, based on their particular situations. The goals must be achievable and attainable, while simultaneously getting them to stretch.

For some, if they work for a company and have a certain amount of vacation time they haven't used, ask them to consider using some of that vacation time to really launch their business.

That said, some people won't come along.

They just won't

You will almost certainly find that some people can't/won't get on board. Understand it and accept it. Fighting it only makes things worse. But you do need to assess how many people *are* going to get on board and to what degree. And if they can't commit to going full-out for the entire 90 days, that's okay, too. Perhaps they can do 30 days? Or 60 days?

And what about you? You might still be in a job yourself. Even if you're only working the business part time, you can still do a 90-day plan. Remember, in my case, many of the years that I worked in network marketing, I did it at night after I got off work. When I got home, I would go back in my back room and would pick up that phone and start pounding.

You can do the same thing. The key is consistency. Even if you can only do one to two hours per day, the key is doing it consistently. When you get home from your job, that's when your career begins. Besides, some people can get more done part time than full time because they make sure their time is focused on the most productive activities.

The 4ᵗʰ Principle: Respect

The principle of respect has to do with understanding the goals of others. The basis of this principle is that you respect that your goals are not *their* goals—your goals are *your* goals.

Respecting your people means talking to them to find out what their goals are. Most of them probably have financial goals, but do they have a goal for achieving a certain rank? Volume goals? What about goals for recognition? Some people just want to be up on stage giving a speech. Find out what *they* want to accomplish during the three months of the plan.

The 5ᵗʰ Principle: Timing

The principle of timing has to do with the reality that people will be on different energy cycles. That's the beauty of a 90-day plan. It's designed for people to use a burst of energy, to do what they need to do to get the business to the next plateau.

And people will be at different places in their business development. Some will have been in the business for years. Others will just be starting. You'll need to adjust your plan as the 90 days proceed, to work with something that's always changing.

The Three-Month Breakdown

The 90-Day Plan is divided into three 30-day periods.

Month One:

The first month is all about finding leaders to join your team. *(Again, I use the term "leaders" to describe anyone interested in building a business, no matter how new they are.)*

In this month, 80 percent of your time will be spent prospecting and recruiting, with the other 20 percent of your time spent on training the new people who have come aboard.

Also, during that first month, you'll need to start the process of identifying and working with six drivers. This number may be lower than six, of course, if you can't find that many. But six is the ideal number.

So, what's a *driver?*

Drivers are people who are serious about growing their business fast. In my case, that meant people like me. They wanted to go hard and fast, just like I did.

My overall strategy was to focus the lion's share of my time developing these six drivers—*but first I needed to find them.* And that required massive action in terms of prospecting and recruiting because I might need to prospect 100 people to find my six.

Find Out Who They Know

Once you identify the six drivers, spend time speaking with each of them to find out who they know. The goal is to tap into each person's warm market—the people with whom they already have relationships. People who already know them, like them, trust them, and are most likely to agree to listen to the opportunity.

From my experience, a person's warm market is always the fastest way to create growth, especially during the first 30 days. And, in situations where one doesn't see much in terms of results in the first month, don't panic. You're laying the foundation of your business. And, just like construction workers laying the foundation of a building, the building itself won't be immediately visible. But when the building starts to go up, it will appear as if it went up overnight.

Month Two:

During month two, you shift your time from 80 percent prospecting to 80 percent supporting your six key drivers. The second month is all about duplication.

Here's the way I do it:

I work with one of my six drivers for an entire day. For example, Driver #1 on Monday, Driver #2 on Tuesday, etc. This means that over a six-day period, I've spent a full, dedicated day with each of my six drivers. I take Sundays off.

Remember, we're only talking about six drivers here, not 60 or 600. So don't flip out thinking you can't do this—*you can.* Anybody can do this.

Keep an Organized Schedule

The key thing is, I maintained an organized schedule for my drivers. For example: On Monday, I'd be with John, helping him make presentations to prospective customers and (ideally) prospective leaders. These presentations may be in someone's living room, at a coffee shop, on a three-way call and/or online.

It doesn't matter. What matters is they know I'm available for them the entire day.

John knows that *every Monday for four weeks* I'm going to be working with *him*, which lets him plan and schedule for it.

I have a different person I work with on Tuesdays, a different driver on Wednesdays, and so on. I help them make lists of people they know who might be interested in using the products and/or building a network marketing business.

Make People Self-Sufficient

During this 30-day period, my drivers get to watch me make presentations and see how I explained the features and benefits of the product, the compensation plan, and answer common questions. All of it. And, as they became comfortable with the process, I'd let them take the lead. In that way, I wasn't doing the work *for* them—I was doing it *with* them. They were getting trained as we went.

After that month, each leader had seen me do a presentation a minimum of four times and by the end of month two, they were as good at making presentations as I was. Now they're thinking, *"Okay, I think I can really do this!"*

Though I was working a full day, dedicated to a single driver, each of the six knew I would make myself available to any of them (schedule permitting) should they need to ask a question or do a three-way call. This not only made them more comfortable, it also allowed me to maximize my time.

The Goal for the Second Month

I had one goal to aim for by the end of the second month, and that was for each of my six drivers to recruit six drivers, duplicating exactly what I'd done during my first month.

With this as the goal, two things happen:

1. *My six drivers get excited because they're making great progress building <u>their</u> teams, and...*

2. *They don't want to quit.*

That's right, *they don't quit.*

Contrary to popular belief, the main reason most people quit the business isn't the fear of failure and rejection—it's lack of progress. Think about it: if 10 people told you they weren't interested (in other words, they said "no" to you), but you also signed up six who said "yes" and you started making money, you'd probably keep going. But if no one signs up and all you've done is spend money, you simply wouldn't have the faith that it was going to work so you'd probably be out.

Quick progress is critical.

Discover Who Is <u>Really</u> Committed

One other thing. By the end of the second month, you're really going to see which of your drivers is truly, absolutely committed to growing their business and, therefore, worthy of your time.

When I do a 90-day plan, I am absolutely, 100 percent committed to my leaders. But commitment is a two-way street. I'm giving everything I have to their success, and I expect them to be just as dedicated to their success. I hold them accountable to the goals they set for themselves when we started working together.

And if they won't hold up their end of the bargain? If I'm showing up but they aren't? I'm going to give them hell, I promise you that. They better show up, because that's what they agreed to do. I remind people of their dreams *they* told me mattered to them, and I do everything I can to force them into action.

And if they still don't keep their promises, the promises they've made to me and to themselves? Then that's it, I'm out.

Month Three:

During the third month of the 90-day plan, I work with my six main drivers to help them develop the six driver's they've brought on board. Once I've got those 36 leaders duplicating themselves, I identify the people who are truly on board with a 90-day plan and form an "inner circle group" just for that.

This can be done via conference calls, or you can create a private Facebook group where people can meet, interact, push each other, and discuss what's happening—sharing encouragement and, if necessary, asking each other for help.

Yes, you've got to continue to support your people like crazy, but nothing says you have to do all the heavy lifting yourself.

Work Through Your Leaders

The 90-day plan isn't simply about accomplishing what you want; it's about accomplishing what you want by helping others accomplish what *they* want. You do not want to get to the end of a 90-day plan to discover you've achieved your goals, but most of your leaders have not achieved theirs. That's why, during my 90-day push, I held a call every day to make sure everyone was on track with their goals.

Celebration and Recognition

When I got to the end of my first 90-day plan, I broke out the champagne and celebrated. As part of your 90-day plan, you want to figure out how you're going to celebrate and recognize people for their achievements. What's sad is my upline was so jealous of the numbers my team had achieved that they not only refused to acknowledge my accomplishment, they refused to talk to me at our first convention. It hurt, but it said more about *them* than it did about me.

Priscilla Smith taught me about the huge importance of recognition. I was up in Bangor, Maine and excited about being at a recognition and celebration event she planned. I was there to give a speech to motivate the leaders. When I got there she said, *"Glad you're here, look forward to hearing from you, but why don't you just take that seat there because we're going to recognize our leaders first."*

I watched the ceremony and saw people being given ribbons for doing as little as $300 in sales volume. It was really smart on the part of that team's leadership. But, more than that, it made me realize how those people had driven 2-3 hours to the meeting just to get that ribbon!

As Napoleon said:

> **"Give me enough ribbons to place on the tunics of my soldiers, and I can conquer the world."**

Never underestimate the importance recognition plays in team performance. Recognize everyone at your celebration events, no matter how small the achievement.

You may even want to have your own special celebration (a lunch, dinner, whatever) at the conclusion of your 90-day plan. If you want to blow it up big, you can have your own "mini-convention" and get a few guest speakers to present.

90 Days Can Change Your Life

Success never comes from individual performance alone. It is always the result of surrounding yourself with a talented team of people who share common goals and values but possess talents that compensate and offset your weaknesses. Having a strong, focused, all-out 90-day push is the best way to build your team. And if you give it everything you've got, those 90-days can change your life.

They changed mine.

During my 90-day plan, I worked 16 hours per day, every day, without stopping. As I mentioned, I like to joke that I worked from *"eight to faint."*

Yes, it was "crazy," but sometimes it takes being a bit crazy to get things done. My crazy 90-day run created a sense of urgency in both myself and others, and it created a ripple effect that has continued to this day—*over 20 years later.*

"When the mountain calls your name, you have only two choices—ignore it and stay in the shade of the valley or put on your shoes and climb."

— Jeff Altgilbers

PART TEN:

Time to Start YOUR Climb

I f you've been in the business a few years and have achieved a level of success, it's easy to become complacent. It's easy to think that once you reach a certain level, that you're set. Then things start to slip—slowly, subtly and so slightly that you don't even notice at first. Then, suddenly you're not ranking like you did in the past.

If this is the case, you must get back involved in the business and get out of the "success coma."

When I bought our mountain home, it was 4,500 square feet. Then we decided to do a 6,500 square foot addition. The problem was the foundation for the addition needed to be different than the foundation of the original house.

When you look at any building, two-thirds of the weight of that building is below ground, in the foundation. Believe it or not, an experienced builder can watch the cement being poured at a construction site, and they can tell you how tall the building is going to be.

For those of you who have been in network marketing for a while, your business has a foundation to it. So you can't just decide one day to grow a bigger business and do it with an old foundation. See what I mean? You've got to dig deep before you can build up.

So how deep does your foundation have to be? It depends on how big your dream is and where you want to get to.

Don't Waste Time Comparing Yourself to Others

Admittedly, some forms of comparison can be healthy—looking up to certain people, admiring their positive qualities and skills, for the purposes of duplicating their methods for achieving success. This is a healthy form of comparison, something referred to as *modeling*.

Modeling is a proven shortcut to success.

The problem is when people look at the top earners in their company and doubt themselves, thinking, *"How will I ever be able to catch up with them?"* The reality is: You don't need to catch up to them, and there's a chance you never will.

I'm very proud to have been recognized as one of the Top 100 MLM income earners of the world (ranked #70 at the time of this writing) but have no illusion that I will ever become number one. Or even in the top 25, or even the top 50. Maybe I will, maybe I won't. I don't care. Because a single minute spent comparing myself to others is a minute that could be spent building my business and/or enjoying the life I do have, not getting distracted by the lives of others.

How much food do you need to eat? How many items of clothing are you going to wear? How many cars do you need to drive? How many houses do you need to own before you're going to be happy?

I feel I've been blessed with more than I deserve, and here's what I know:

You will get enough and be enough if you do enough.

You don't have to be like your upline or the superstar who was on the stage last month at the convention. You've got nothing to prove to anyone.

Comparison Versus Competition

It's important to not confuse comparison with competition. Competition can be good as long as it's coming from a healthy place. When I joined my company 20 years ago, they sang the praises of a particular leader quite often. To be honest, I got tired of comparing myself to her. So I decided to stop *comparing* and decided to start *competing*. There's a big difference.

Do you know why they put blinders on racehorses? They put blinders on racehorses because they don't want the horses looking at the other horses. They don't want them to get distracted. They want them look forward, at where they're going, not to the see what the other horses are doing.

Put your blinders on and just run *your* race.

And if You Ever Think About Quitting...

Do *you* ever think about quitting? I did.

So many times, I thought maybe I'm not cut out for this and maybe this is not for me. I'm not this and I'm not that. I'm no salesperson and I'm not a presenter because I don't want to get up in front of a meeting room and talk to people.

When we find ourselves having these inner conversations, it's usually because we are experiencing a disappointment of some kind. It's never when things are going great. It's never when we're experiencing victories.

When you find yourself experiencing moments of doubt, stop and reflect on why you got involved in network marketing in the first place. Was it for money? Freedom? Pride? Security? Why did you start? People refer to this as *finding your why.*

But, here's the thing:

> *Finding your "why" is how you motivate*
> *yourself to start. Remembering your why*
> *is how you keep going.*

When moments of doubt and frustration present themselves, it's very important to reflect on the reason/reasons you started this journey in the first place. And if you quit, what then?

Where does that put you?

Something led you here, to this profession. *To this possibility.* Something you could not find out there in the "corporate" world. So, what was it? What was it that appealed to you?

Whatever it was that you couldn't find, you can find and will find it here.

If...

You...

Don't...

Quit.

Network Marketing Is Not "Easy"...

I never tell anyone who joins my team that network marketing is *easy*. It isn't. I tell them it's simple...*because it is.* The process of inviting people to buy your products and consider an opportunity, and then to show how to share the same opportunity with others, is simple—*it couldn't be any simpler!* That's the best part of what network marketing has to offer.

But *simple* is not the same as *easy.*

It's not "easy."

...But It <u>Is</u> Worth It!

Ask anyone who's ever stuck with it long enough to succeed, and they'll tell you. And, like I'm doing right now, they'll tell you not to quit. They'll also tell you that it gets easier. The more you do and the longer you persist, the easier it gets.

And in those moments of doubt and frustration, when things aren't going your way, understand that it's not going to be easier somewhere else.

Impact Before Income

It's been a 40-year journey, and the people I've met in so many countries I've had the good fortune to travel to have provided me with enough memories for three lifetimes. And there's not a day that goes by where I am not grateful, and thank God, for the many blessings He has given me and my family.

And we'd like to think that *we* have impacted other families around the world in the same way others have impacted ours. Because, when everything is said and done, *impact is more important than income.* But, if you play your cards right, *you can achieve both.*

A Final Thought Before Parting...

Forgive me if this comes across as a bit of a *rant* (and perhaps a strange way to end this book) but after all these years, it still kills me when I see that people will get up early in the morning, drop the kids off at school or daycare, fight rush-hour traffic to get to a job that pays too little, and work all day with people who don't appreciate them.

Then those same people fight their way back home through that same traffic, cook dinner, and plop themselves down in front of the TV, feeling burned out and exhausted, hoping to wind down and relax for an hour or two, desperately trying to escape the stress of their lives.

And then, 24 hours later, even though they know they're merely living an existence rather than a life, they'll get up and do it all over again.

And again.

And again.

Over and over, every single day, until they're old and gray. Until they're completely worn down by a life that was never the life they truly wanted. I never considered that as a plan for happiness.

And neither should you.

The truth is, millions of people enter the network marketing profession every year, yet not everyone succeeds. The question is *why?* Why do so many people fail?

It is my belief, after 40 years working in this profession, that there are two reasons:

- *The number-one reason people fail is because they were not properly mentored by an effective leader who could show them the way.*

- *The second reason is a lack of patience, expecting results to show up without giving the system a chance to work* for them.

The system works, if you're willing to work the system.

Time to climb.

Also available from
Success in 100 Pages publishing...

Available in Kindle, paperback and audio at
Amazon.com

About the Author...

Jeff Altgilbers is an eight-figure income earner with over 700,000 distributors in 57 countries in his downline. Success didn't come easy or fast, and even with years of struggle and near poverty, he didn't give up on his network marketing dream. After selling his broken-down truck to a junk man, he took some of the money and invested it into product to start up his business. Today, Jeff Altgilbers is one of the top-100 income earners in the world of network marketing and is proud to have over 100 millionaires in his downline. He has spoken all over the world for his company conventions, as well as at network marketing events for top trainers like Eric Worre and Ray Higdon.

Jeff lives in Gatlinburg, Tenn. in his dream home in the mountains with his wife, Michelle, and two sons. They travel together often, visiting their teams all over the world. And when not playing music, entertaining at his home, or watching bears play in his front yard, you can probably find Jeff online mentoring people, giving advice and providing encouragement, as well as inspiring anyone who wants to achieve their goals

within the network marketing profession. As Jeff is fond of saying, *"The secret to success is to not keep your success a secret!"*

Jeff can be found at: <u>JeffAltgilbers.com</u>

Lightning Source UK Ltd.
Milton Keynes UK
UKHW020201250220
359246UK00008B/304